GOOD TOGETHER

A Journey Through Relationships

Jerry Brook

Innovative Ingenuity Press
Houston, Texas
2017

Innovative Ingenuity Press
Houston, Texas

ISBN's
Perfect Binding — 978-0-9973485-0-7
eBook/.MOBI — 978-0-9973485-1-4
eBook/.ePub — 978-0-9973485-2-1

www.JerryBrook.com
www.GoodTogether.com

Book Packager and Project Coordinator — Rita Mills
Editor & Collaborator — Faye Walker
Cover Design — Laura Hidalgo

Printed in The United States of America

Dedication

This book is dedicated to "You", the reader. I may not know each and every one of you personally, but I do know a thing or two about you.

You, like me, have had relationships, some of which have failed. You, like me, have wondered, "what went wrong?", "what could I have done differently?", and "will I ever be able to figure any of this out?".

I dedicate this work to your courage to continuing to seek out the answers to those questions. Because it is only by; getting involved, making choices, and not leaving it up to chance, that you can succeed in any of your endeavors.

———⋅◆⋅———

Table of Contents

Acknowledgments

This book is a work of a great amount of; time, effort, and sacrifice. It represents significant aspects of my life.

There are two facets to any book, the physical production and the emotional foundation. Each facet encompasses a number of people, both positively and negatively.

Each and every one of these people has contributed, in their own way, to the construction of this work.

The list of names would be long, and of no use to anyone. In fact, some of these people would rather remain nameless.

Too all of you, both positive and negative, I thank each and every one of you, you know who you are. And if anyone asks, I will tell them that you were one of the positive ones.

Foreword

> *By three methods may we learn wisdom:*
> *First, by reflection, which is noblest;*
> *Second, by imitation, which is easiest; and*
> *Third, by experience, which is the bitterest.*
> —Confucius

I wrote this book because I followed the conventional wisdom, and it failed me. In relationship after relationship—personal and business—I came to see I was using bad advice to make decisions. Being a technically oriented person, I started to examine why certain relationships failed and others flourished, why I made the decisions I made, how I followed through and why. I came to believe that most conventional wisdom is "conventional" because it has been around for a long, long time, but that doesn't make it good or right.

Bad advice and misconceptions about relationships—of all kinds—come from quixotic sayings, the "experts," and our culture. But it often fails to take into consideration the most important maxim, "Know yourself." Now this is good advice, but most people don't even know how to understand their ways of thinking and making decisions. This book walks you through the various aspects of relationships, with an emphasis on decision making so you can not only "Know yourself," but others as well.

My personal path has been first imitation, that was doing what I thought I saw others doing, which was easiest; second was experience, that was doing what others had advised me to do, which was bitterest; and lastly was reflection, that was actually thinking about what I could have, or should have, done.

You will discover this book is written somewhat unconventionally. We've been taught to think in a linear way. Stories move from beginning to middle to end. However, our minds actually reach in many directions at a time; our thoughts are like a web, wherein one thought leads to several which, in turn, lead to several more. The World Wide Web uses this idea at its foundation. Most books treat topics as a hierarchy, from the top down: first do this, then do that, and so on. But a useful discussion of relationships is not structured so neatly. In *Good Together*, I explore a few major concepts and then add to them or build upon them or apply them to other areas of our lives. This additive nature gives the book more of a web-like reference. Certain ideas will show up again and again because I discuss them from multiple perspectives. Repetition is not only how we learn, but how we think, and I want this book to represent a different way of approaching the topic.

What this means for you is that every chapter details some aspect of a *Good Together* relationship, but you may come upon that information from a different perspective as you read through the book. If I could write a material book like a web, I would have. That seems to me most true for the information I have to impart. But reading is linear and books are linear, so the cumulative approach seemed to fit most perfectly with my way of thinking about and acting on relationships.

This book is meant to be gender neutral because, as you shall see, all or most of the items apply equally. I challenge the current stereotypes—"Women do this" and "Men do that"—which often lean on misapplied science and advice. Therefore, the pronouns "he," "she," or "they" are used as convention (in the royal sense) and for ease of use and understanding. They can, however, be interchanged.

In a sense, this is a companion book to the information I engage on the website. I encourage you to visit me there and learn more about decision-making, commitment, fear, and other topics I will pursue.

Here we go.

Introduction

Good Together is not like other relationship books. I won't tell you what to do. I will show you how to know yourself, recognize types and phases of relationships, make your own decisions, and create meaningful relationships with family, friends, colleagues, and intimates.

So what does Good Together mean? You probably already know: the boss and employee who know how to build a project together almost without speaking, partners in the kitchen who move seamlessly from one job to another to produce an elegant meal, partners who finish one another's sentences and then laugh about it.

The concept of Good Together represents union, a cohesive connection, a bond that goes beyond simply participating in activities, but extends to having a common goal, purpose and understanding.

This book, *Good Together,* covers aspects of all relationships, social, business, intimate. It is about finding, forging, and maintaining the best relationships possible within the range of people you have contact with. It offers a unique and unconventional view of relationships and the people in them so that we can make them more solid, comprehensive, and long-lasting.

Our entire lives, from adolescence, through middle age, and into old age are all about relationships. So why haven't we figured out how to manage them successfully? Why are we always running up against one another, falling out with family, friends and co-workers, leaving and joining new intimate relationships?

You're reading this book because some relationship or aspect of relationship has disappointed you. Well, don't feel bad. The truth is we haven't been taught properly about relationships. After all, which class have you taken or been offered which broaches the subject? My intention is to assist you in learning the answers—not my answers, but your personal answers.

The most used, and abused, excuse of all times is the phrase "It's complicated." We use it especially when dealing with relationships. It is so prevalent there is a movie titled, you know, It's Complicated. Haven't we all heard or said it at one time or another? Simply put it translates to:

- It's none of your business;
- It's too painful to discuss;
- I don't want to take the time, expend the effort, and make the sacrifice, necessary to deal with this situation;
- I don't want to face what I intuitively, internally, know to be true because that would disrupt the status quo and potentially cause distress.

This book attempts to demystify a subject about which most people would throw their hands in the air and exclaim, "It's complicated." It simply isn't as complex, or complicated, as people make it out to be. The more complex or convoluted people assume relationships are, the more you will need to rely on someone for advice. They want you to believe it is "too complicated" for you, the general public, to understand; therefore, you need the wizards, the mystics, the experts. But it is either low self-esteem or lack of the necessary education which makes you believe you are not smart enough or others are smarter. You can easily understand what it takes to make a good relationship: first, the individual parts of a relationship, and second how those pieces fit together (good together, that is).

So it isn't complicated.

I'm going to refer throughout this book to the many types of relationships we participate in: social, having to do with family, friends, acquaintances, and intimates—sometimes lovers and sometimes not—as well as business types, such as employer, employee, coworkers, and other commercial transactions. All these relationships have phases although not all phases are necessarily in every relationship: the beginning, coming together, the middle, the mine field, and the end, moving apart. And all of these relationships have common factors, the most obvious one being you, yourself.

You've probably heard the maxim, "Know yourself." It's true. The problem is most people don't know themselves. In fact, they don't really know their values, their desires, their needs, their wishes for the future. They might not even know or understand their pasts, which have shaped them. How many times have you thought, asked, or been asked, "Can we really know another person?" If we don't know ourselves, then how can we expect anyone else to know us? And vice versa. If they don't know themselves, then the answer is simple, "We cannot possibly know them." We simply don't take the time nor do we have a road map needed to know ourselves, much less someone else. We need to prepare ourselves for relationships, not simply dive into them or let the current take us where it may.

All relationships are an adventure. The first thing we must do is determine the destination. Without knowing the destination, we wander aimlessly. With the destination in mind, we can determine what we must do to reach our goals. Once we know the relationship we are looking for, the next thing we must do is prepare for it. You wouldn't climb a mountain without the proper planning and expertise, so why enter into a relationship without a sufficient strategy? Where are you headed?

Here's the essential piece we start with: the preparation we need for relationships is to understand people. We start by understanding ourselves: where we've been, where we are now, and where we're going. Then we accept that those same rules apply to everyone in the relationship.

Once we know our destination and have done our preparation, we need to take the journey, which is the individual interactions we have with others, how we communicate with others and how we interpret their attempts at communication with us, also known as relationships. We can't take a journey without a destination. That's simply roaming. You won't know when you've arrived or when you should feel satisfied because you won't have a goal. While you're on your journey, others may also be on their own journeys. A word of caution: if one person is on a journey—with a destination in mind—and the other person is simply roaming, then they can't be headed to the same place. Do you see how this journey is an interaction? It is dynamic; it's a two-way street.

This book is going to focus on relationships and the people in them. Sounds simple, and rest assured I will make it so because it isn't as complex or complicated as you have been led to believe. But I want you to figure out "what" you and they do and "why" you and they do it. And rather than focusing on one type of relationship or on one of the stages of a relationship like others before have done, this book deals with a wide range of relationships and experiences. After all, that's what we do every day, involve ourselves in many different kinds of relationships at all different stages with a variety of people. I have come to understand these different kinds of relationships, business, social, and family, all have things in common. So in some cases, when we are having difficulty determining what to do, we can use other relationship types we are more familiar with as templates.

I aim to help you recognize what you already know.

This book is for people who want to learn about people, themselves as well as others. And it is especially for those who want to learn how to communicate and interact with others, whether in business, family, friendships or intimate relationships. Personal relationships don't exist without people, and they can't happen without interaction. Therefore, people and their interactions constitute, create, and define relationships.

You may wonder why I wrote this book. I'm not a psychologist, economist, business strategist, or fancy Ph.D. therapist. I'm a person much like you, who, after yet another failed intimate relationship, reflected on my past and reevaluated all the folk wisdom and professional advice I had received and tried to apply. And, as a consequence, I came to see that the advice and conventional wisdom didn't actually work. If it did, we would all be much better off than we presently are. I realized I didn't agree with much conventional wisdom, or conventions themselves; therefore, by definition, I am unconventional. At times, being unconventional means being controversial, and, at times, being controversial means being confrontational. In this book, I want to confront those things which are unpopular in order to help you learn what is best for you and to help you feel comfortable in your relationships.

Furthermore, I will show you, not tell you, what is best for you in your relationships. I want to teach you how to make your own advice (decisions) so you can stop listening to others. Their intentions may be good, but their understanding of relationships and the people in them is poor.

Because of my background in working with computers and my analytical nature, which I employ every day, I am very adept at following directions or instructions. Therefore, I came to understand it wasn't that I was misapplying the advice, rather it was the advice itself that was not correct or practical. In trying to understand people, I used my analytical, logical, rational skills to research problems, gather pertinent information, and try to make sense of it.

Follow me to the road map.

———◦◦◦———

SECTION I

Good Together

1

Choice Not Chance

"Choice not chance" means understanding the decision-making processes in order for you to better understand my conclusions, and so you, too, may be able to come to your own conclusions.

My research began with Artificial Intelligence, which led to the need to understand decision making, which led to understanding people, their personalities and their behaviors, an endeavor which has taken more years than I like to admit.

Artificial Intelligence is actually a misnomer. What exactly is intelligence? Is there a difference if it issues from a human or a machine? If a young child knows to take an umbrella when there looks to be a chance of rain, we think that process is intelligence. A computer can be programmed to come to the same conclusion. Since both use the same or similar criteria to make their determination, and since they both come to the same conclusion, the intelligence isn't different or artificial. A major component of intelligence is making good decisions; however, that is not to say the *correct* decisions.

What do I mean by that? The idea that all things can be expressed as being correct or incorrect is a flawed or false understanding. When I was younger, I believed there was one and only one right answer to any given question, and everything else was wrong. I call this the "Best Principle," and I am not alone in my understanding. Most people believe there is only one right answer because school teaches us to think this way. However, I've learned that isn't always the case.

In my job, I work with customers to specify and choose which equipment they need in order to meet their particular requirements. The customers and I didn't always agree on the choices. Why? I viewed things strictly from a technical standpoint. Over time, I have come to realize that in many cases there isn't actually a clear technical winner when choosing between options. In some cases, the choice has so many variables that the final decision depends on the importance placed on each of the individual attributes. In my business, variables such as cost, schedule, reliability, ease of operation, and availability of support are as important as the equipment itself. In some cases, the final choice was not technical at all; it was a question of personal preference. Helping customers understand they may be choosing a product based on hidden criteria or values has helped me make better sense of decision-making and "intelligence."

There is no correct, universal, or technical answer to "What flavor of ice cream do you like?" It is a personal, or individual, preference. The same question may have different conclusions depending on things such as different objectives, different perspectives, different starting points, or different foundations.

In other words, there are many shades of gray.

Many decisions are driven by both the situation as well as the people in the situation. For example, the quantity of risk you should accept in your retirement investments varies over time, from a young worker who has a great deal of time to save and therefore might be open to greater risk to the older worker who is close to retirement and feels he or she cannot tolerate risk. There simply isn't a singular, universal, correct answer to the question "How much risk should I take?" Your "foundation"—your background, the way you interpret, view, or relate to the details of the situation—as well as the information you have available greatly influences the decisions you make. So why is it important we understand intelligence and decision-making? Everything we do is a decision of some kind, whether or not it is conscious or intentional.

Choice, not chance. It is your life, your relationships; you are involved. The question is "To what extent?"

Relationships are personal. Only you can know what is best for you. And with my help, through this book and my website, you can discover the best decisions for yourself. You can determine your own destinations, prepare yourself, plot a course, take a journey, and maintain and sustain your relationships.

———•◆•———

2
CHAPTER

The Benefits of Decisions

I learned from researching Artificial Intelligence there is a concept called the Availability Heuristic: you tend to believe anecdotes and news stories are more representative of the big picture than they actually are, that they are not just isolated incidents. For example, if you see several news stories featuring shark attacks, you might think sharks are increasingly violent. Actually, the news is simply covering them a lot more. So we learn from what information is at hand. We explore and investigate using that information (that's where the word "heuristic" comes from).

Thoughts, and the succeeding decisions we make, are often based on the information at hand while ignoring additional, pertinent information which may exist. Hindsight Bias is similar. You have thoughts and make current decisions based on what you know now, not based on what you knew at the time you made the decision. That's why we say, "If only I knew then what I know now."

People use this focused, or selective, view of reality in making decisions about intimate relationships, too. When people only remember the good times, or when they play up the success of couplings, or down play the numerous failures, they are using the Availability Heuristic. People are optimistic about their relationships. Why not? We all want the best for ourselves. So we assume, or more correctly, we hope, our relationships will work, without giving any thought to "why" they would or even should work.

In one study, researchers examined the recognition process; they wanted to discover its effect on the ability of individuals to recall relevant past experiences they could use to improve future task performance with practice. The researchers wanted to know if decision makers recognize (past) situations, and if so, whether decision making performance correlates with an increase in similarity between current and past decisions. They also wanted to know which factors influenced recognition and how those factors changed as performance improved. Researchers monitored individual decisions and determined similarity of decisions across the trials.

Good performers, people who recognized or remembered past situations, showed higher than average decision-making skills from the very beginning. In general, what researchers found was the recognition process contributes to the type of experience individuals accumulate as they work to complete a dynamic task.

Dynamic Decision-Making tasks require that multiple and interdependent decisions be made in an environment which changes in response to a decision-maker's actions. So, as experience accumulates, decision makers become more selective, adjust their decisions, and gradually change the task features that trigger the response. What this means in real life is making decisions and evaluating those decisions leads to better decisions in the future, just as sports repetition builds muscle memory. Learn by doing. On the other hand, not making your own decisions— taking the advice of others—leads to dependence, not learning how to go about making one's own decisions. In order to make good future decisions, people must be able to relate the current situation with similar past events.

Another study looked at ethical decision-making and performance of organizational managers. They discovered high performing teams made more ethical decisions than low performing teams. Past performance, evaluation, and repetition can correct and reinforce both the ability to make decisions and the quality of those decisions. Positive reinforcement is a confidence builder.

There was no evidence to support that age played a significant role in ethical decision- making. The ability to envision the similarities of the situations mattered most. If a person's ethical convictions are consistent, their decisions should also be consistent. In other words, a lack of convictions leads to inconsistent decisions, as well as inconsistent behaviors.

Your need for good decision-making rests on understanding the similarities between different relationships as well as various situations within those relationships. This is what I aim to show you.

Now, it is important to recognize decision-making is not the same as problem solving. A group usually makes a decision in one of four ways: (1) authoritarian, where the leader makes the decision and it is assumed to be final, such as a judge handing down a decision in a courtroom; (2) sub-group, in which a small part of the team gains significant influence and forces a decision, such as in politics when a vocal minority, with nothing to lose, refuses to budge or cooperate with the majority. The majority, which desires some resolution, then is coerced into concessions.

(3) The majority rules where, as the name implies, the majority determines the outcome. There are many downsides to this method, some obvious and some unapparent. As many as close to half of all the participants may disagree. In the case where there are more than two choices or options, the outcome may not reflect the true desire of the majority. In a three-party race, for example, some people may vote for the candidate who has no actual chance of winning as a show of overall dissatisfaction with the system. The outcome may be that the candidate they truly did not want to win actually wins. So not only were their votes in vain, they allowed the scales to be tipped away from what would have been their second choice.

(4) Decisions are also made by consensus in which everyone must agree before a decision is reached. In practice, this may be very difficult for a variety of reasons, one of which is significant influence by a sub-group.

In the cases of using sub-group, majority rules and consensus to reach a decision, studies have shown it can take as little as five percent of the people to influence a group. That statistic suggests all these techniques are susceptible to the minority, and, therefore, it is fair to ask whether these outcomes or decisions made are reasonable because we use our personalities—qualities like charm, cunning, and confidence—to influence others just as they use their personalities to influence us.

So what does this have to do with relationships? In part, it shows conventional wisdom, advice and expert opinions are all susceptible to such things as sub-groups' influence, and majority or consensus adherence (that is, going along with the crowd) rather than focusing on and accepting facts, regardless of what they may be.

How Personality Affects Decision-Making

In order to understand decision-making, why we make the decisions we do, and why they might be different from person to person and situation to situation, I needed to understand people. So I began by researching what we call personalities.

Two of the most common and popular personality models or "tests" are the Big Five and the Myers Briggs Temperament Index, but I found I couldn't entirely agree with either of them. Using my knowledge of proper analysis and decision-making, I found flaws in all the personality models I researched. The existing philosophy upon which these tests are founded is to categorize the outward appearance of how people act and the effects those actions may have. The problems with this philosophy are twofold: first, these responses are only a portion of what makes up people and their personalities; and second, it ignores the motivations *behind* the actions.

My dissatisfaction with the models led me to the need to understand people's motivations. But in order to understand motivations, I had to understand human behavior: what it is and where it comes from. I had to create my own model of people, their personalities, their motivations, and their interactions in order to understand people more thoroughly. I also realized people, lay people as well as supposed experts, either don't understand or don't apply decision-making processes and techniques to the subject of relationships, the lack of which contributes, in large part, to the high failure rate.

Around the time I was putting all of this information together, I went through yet another failed intimate relationship. I decided to see if I could apply what I had learned to relationships.

I was astounded by what I found.

———•◆•———

$$3$$

Preparing for the Journey

Why Can't You Find a Relationship?

You can't find a relationship or succeed in one for two good reasons: 1) because of all the bad, incorrect advice you've taken and 2) because you don't know "who you are and what you want" or "who others are and what they want."

Imagine you are opening a business, a store. You don't know what you are selling or the service you are providing. You don't know what you have in inventory, and, therefore, you don't know what to charge, what the value is, of the goods or services. Since you don't know what you are selling, you also don't know "who" your customers will be. You don't know what they will want, you don't know how much they will offer for, or value, your services, or products, and you don't know if what they offer is worth it to you.

In other words, you don't know yourself, what you have to offer a relationship, and what the value is of what you have to offer. At the same time, you don't know "who" may want what you are offering, or if you want what they are offering in return. You can't know if they value you or if you value them.

Have you ever noticed when people go to a party, they don't typically bring anything? People expect the Host to provide all the food, the spirits, and the entertainment. Once the food or spirits run out, or when they no longer enjoy the entertainment, they leave the party. These people never stay around to help you clean up.

They're "just there for the beer!"

I can't tell you the number of women I have dated who believe I am the Host and it is up to me to provide the entertainment. They simply show up, with hardly anything to offer, and expect me to provide everything for the relationship, all the fun, excitement, joy, pleasure, and so on. They invest very little of themselves. Once they have had their fill, they get bored and either they expect me to change, or they find another party. They leave me to clean up any of the mess.

Having a Destination

I suggested earlier you have to determine your destination before you set out on a relationship. You wouldn't leave your house without having somewhere to go. If you have nowhere to go, how will you know when you get there? If you have no goal to achieve, then how will you ever know when you have reached it?

Most people don't ask the right questions when they begin a relationship. Some don't ask any at all. Too many relationships arise from the path of least resistance. We start relationships with the people who surround us and not from an active effort on our part. Relationships too often are not thought out or planned in any way and not directed towards anyone in particular. People are so set on having a relationship they sacrifice everything else for, or in the name of, the relationship.

So why do people end up in the relationships they do? Relationship Coach Stephanie McKenzie has been in the coaching business for several years. She says, "In the beginning phase of a relationship, people don't ask the hard questions; they don't undertake their due diligence."

People use themselves as the yardsticks. They want to believe if I like rock and roll and I like you, then you, too, must like rock and roll; I don't even need to ask. Some people don't even want to ask if the relationship is exclusive. They would rather assume the best, than deal with the worst.

The conventional wisdom of the necessity for sacrifice, compromise, and hard work in order to make a relationship allows people to accept any relationship, with almost any person. That's what people think a relationship is: you putting it above yourself and everything else, so everything becomes about the relationship. If that were the case, you could be in a relationship with anyone because you and the person are not important compared to The Relationship. Many people are looking for any relationship, not for the person, but because they don't want to be alone and lonely.

But all relationships are not created equally, and one size definitely does not fit all.

———•◆•———

4
CHAPTER

How are Relationships Categorized?

W e talk about relationships in one of three ways. By identifying the people in the relationship, by the objectives of the relationship, or by the intensity of the relationship. By being aware of the possible patterns, you can recognize when they're happening to you.

The people in a relationship: We use terms such as Parent—Child, Husband—Wife, Boyfriend—Girlfriend, Employer—Employee, and so on. No two parents, children, husbands, wives, boyfriends, girlfriends, employers, or employees are alike. These descriptors only indicate the people in the relationship.

The objectives of a relationship: We use terms such as marriage, business, partners, religious partnerships, and so on. But not all marriages, businesses, partners, or religious relationships are alike. These descriptors signify the goals, or the function, of the relationship.

The strength of the relationship: We use terms such as acquaintances, friendship, best friends, lovers, soul mates. Again, not all acquaintances, friendships, best friends, lovers, and soul mates are alike. These descriptors measure the bond, or connection, of the relationship.

However, none of these descriptors has an absolutely transparent meaning; they describe aspects of the relationship, not the relationship itself. For example, what does it mean to have a friend or to be a friend?

Are all friendships alike? Of course not; our friendships vary with our situations and the people in those situations, how they act and interact. What about your "friends" on Facebook? Do you have the same kind of relationship with them as the people you see regularly? When my buddy needed help putting his bookshelves together, did he go to his Facebook friends or did he simply call me?

The questions are the same with objectives like "marriage." Your concept of marriage is likely very different from mine because our interpretations are based on our unique past experiences.

These inadequate descriptions are used to define and categorize relationships, so the resulting advice regarding those associations is also incorrect. Well, you say, but surely we can agree on love.

Where did the concept of Romantic Love come from? Why has it taken hold of us so strongly?

Romantic Love?

Understanding the concept of romantic love is important because it dictates the ways in which people act and interact. In our society, romantic love tells us things like how husbands or boyfriends are supposed to, or expected to, act. Why do we have to acknowledge this? It's important to understand that if our expectations are incorrect, then we will continually be disappointed.

What I have found is the idea of romance, as well as the ways in which we express romance, are contrived; they are not dictated by nature but created by humans. This should mean that what passes for romance varies from society to society, and it does; however, with the proliferation of mass media, many societies have merged or tend to mimic aspects of each other.

So when was romance "created"? Prior to the eleventh or twelfth century, the coupling of two individuals was used primarily to join material entities, such as finances or property, or to form a peace treaty. Romance was a thing of fantasy or fiction; it was grounded in myths and legends. Romance was never meant to be put into practice or, if practiced, it was never intended to last. In other words, romance was more synonymous with infatuation, lust, or passion.

In Ancient Greece, marriage was simply cooperation in managing fortune and property. In literature, homosexual love affairs were the closest thing to romantic love. There are many comments on the beauty of boys and accounts of emotional liaisons between men. In fact, women were dismissed and seen as property, while loving another man was viewed as a better, higher-minded, type of love.

Prior to the eleventh century in Europe when depictions of Camelot and King Arthur's court came into fashion, the idea of chivalry and romantic love between a man and a women wasn't written about. Originally, "courtly love" meant to adore or desire a woman from afar. This idea of "true love" was secretive and agonizing and could only be undertaken for a woman one could never marry. The endless difficulties and frustrations of being virtuous were supposed to make a knight a better man, soldier, and Christian.

Rules of Love

At one point, there was an actual "Court of Love," in which the rules of love were defined and debated by Queen Eleanor of Aquitaine. This was a literary convention and probably was never carried out in the queen's court, but the rules suggest a mindset about Romantic Love that has come down to us nearly a thousand years later. The list of thirty-one rules of love included items such as the following:

- The easy attainment of love makes it of little value; difficulty of attainment makes it prized;
- He who is not jealous cannot love;
- A true lover does not desire to embrace in love anyone except his beloved; and
- A true lover considers nothing good except what he thinks will please his beloved.

These tenants of so called love are unrealistic, unreasonable, and immature.

Often, the knight was actually married to another woman. There is a well-documented account of a knight devoting his love to a woman "from afar" for over ten years, while at the same time having a wife and children at home. Romantic love was separated from sex and marriage.

Courtly love, or true love, could include kissing, touching, and fondling, but never intercourse. Intercourse was considered crass or dirty.

What can be surmised, however, is "marrying for love" is fairly recent.

The poets who write longingly of love decry one thing and yet live another; their own lives do not reflect the very love they profess. The "do as I say not as I do" attitude, a bit of wishful thinking, clouds their objectivity. By studying the lives of the poets and writers, we can get some understanding of why they believe the things they do. Some of these people had been abused or neglected beginning in childhood. Their cold treatment by the women in their lives, their mothers generally, severely biased their view of what it is to have a healthy relationship.

This unhealthy, unbalanced view of reality caused an overcompensation for their own low self-esteem and lack of affection. One writer recounted his memories of childhood, describing how his mother died delivering him. His father, who never recovered from the loss, would occasionally set him down and abuse him for having taken the love of his life away. For this man, writing about love was a catharsis, a means to rid himself of the pains of love.

Some of the very people writing of love, and codifying it into the culture, are suffering. Some are dysfunctional, unrealistic, and unreasonable. And yet their bizarre notions are cast in the hearts and minds of society as if they were the mainstream.

Religion plays its part in the coloring of our notion of romantic love. Our society still operates on the extremes of the "Madonna-Whore" dichotomy. On the one hand, we celebrate the wonder of procreation, and on the other hand, we denigrate sex as a sin. Neither of these is romantic love. Therefore, this romantic love must be something different, devoid of sex or intimate touching, love from afar.

This is a type of reversal of cause and effect. When you are separated from the one you love, you have feelings of longing, so by creating a false condition of separation and feelings of longing, you can induce feelings of love. But the deprivation of intimacy is a kind of emotional sadomasochism, a torture of sorts. These poets and writers have confused reality and fantasy.

This view or sentiment of love has been handed down and perpetuated over time, finding its way into modern day fairy tales, which themselves create cultural myths of unconditional love, happily ever after, and so on. If you'll remember, fairy tales often begin with "Once upon a time," the operative word being "once," that is to say, not typically or unusually. What this means is "This will never happen to you."

The stories our culture thrives on are about the anomalies, the unusual. The minority who write the tales, fables, news stories, blogs, and so on are the ones with problems, extreme views, inclinations toward extremes, dysfunction. People who are well-adjusted take for granted their lives are balanced. They may have some ups and downs, but they're not extreme. They have no pressing reason to write about their well-adjusted life.

Soul Mates

In ancient Greek mythology, the gods created man, but once they saw what they had done, they became jealous. The gods split man into two pieces, one man and one woman, creating the concept that leads us to speak of "a better half" and to say, "You complete me." These ideas lead us to the conclusion there is one and only one mate for each person, someone you were split from when you were formed, a "soul" mate.

The use of the word "soul," being a typically religious term, conjures up images of a supernatural, eternal connection. But there are repercussions to these views of soul mate. Once you find your "other half," and since he or she is uniquely and supernaturally connected with you, there is no need for any effort on the parts of the two halves to maintain the relationship. You are just pieces of a puzzle which, once attached, need do nothing more. (Dr. Shauna H. Springer wrote a series about the fallacy of a soul mate but suggests two people married for a long time may develop into something similar.)

Associated with the myth of soul mates is the idea "You can make me happy" or "I can make you happy." But our individual happiness hinges a great deal on our personal satisfaction, comfort, or confidence. Other people are not truly in control of your happiness.

It might be more useful to think of "life mates," which could be many people over the course of a life who move you, shape your thoughts, teach you something.

Suppose you want to purchase a car. You have certain criteria you would like in that car. You want a vehicle which is safe, reliable, stylish, and, of course, within your budget. Very quickly you will discover the safest car isn't the cheapest car, and it also may not be the most stylish car. Safety comes with the tradeoff of the other criteria: safety features cost money, and the safest vehicle may achieve such a title by being large and boxy, which is not very stylish. Similarly, the most reliable car is also not the cheapest car because quality craftsmanship and parts come at a cost. The fact is many items are conflicting with one another; they are all competing for the same resources. The more criteria we list, the more we will have to take into account.

People are no different: at the highest level, we have criteria categorized as physical, emotional, intellectual, and values. No one person can possess, or be, the "best" in all categories. As people excel in one area, they tend to retard in other areas. If you spend all your time in the classroom, intellectual, you are not spending time in the gym, physical, and vice versa.

We also notice there is an interplay among the criteria: a person who may have appeared physically appealing initially may lose some, or all, appeal given his or her emotional or intellectual presentation, and vice versa. In other words, we are always unconsciously balancing, averaging the various criteria. Because of these multiple attributes, various degrees of appeal of each attribute, the interplay between the attributes, and the combination of the attributes, there will be many people, or cars, able to satisfy your goals equally. Too often people get overly focused on a single attribute, or too few attributes, and ignore all of the other attributes. This narrow-mindedness makes finding a satisfying relationship exceedingly difficult. It may cause you to second guess your current choice, jumping from one relationship to another whenever you meet someone you think is better is some specific way.

Many sources point out people tend to say one thing and do something different. One psychologist has calculated for any one person there are at least 50,000 people in the world who could match. Most people will reasonably admit, given that there are billions of people in the world, there must be more than one, and only one, person who would likely be a match. Yet their actions indicate they believe there is one special person just for them, and them alone.

Why Do People "Settle"?

Many people don't take the time to determine what type of relationship they want, what they want from a relationship, what they offer to the relationship, or what they want from the other parties in the relationship. If you don't know what you want, you wouldn't know what you have. You may have the best relationship for yourself, but you wouldn't know it.

Alternatively, you may know exactly what it is you want, but your expectations may be unrealistic. You may want a relationship that is nothing but sunshine. However, nothing but sunshine creates a desert, a dry, desolate, lifeless place. Life requires some rain, a healthy balance between both sun and rain. Rain, challenge, spurs change and growth. Wanting more than is reasonable or realistic leads one to question, "Did I settle?" or to assert, "I can do better."

Choices

In the Middle Ages, there just weren't enough people in the world, let alone in a community one could easily travel to, to worry about whom you were going to marry. Now that we have such a large number of people available to us as potential mates, people suffer from an "analysis paralysis," an information overload. This procrastination brought on by having so many choices makes it difficult to differentiate between all the possible options. Parents know giving a child, or salespeople know giving a customer, too many options leads to confusion, an overwhelming of one's senses. Having a great many potential suitors leads to second guessing. Even after you have made a decision, there is always a nagging doubt: "Was this the 'best' one?" or "Did I settle?"

But the question may be *"Did* you settle?" If you are getting something you want from the relationship, you will likely discount other aspects of the relationship. Only you can determine if what you are getting is of greater value than what you are giving up in return. For instance, if you choose to be in a relationship because the fear of being alone is more important than being happy, then you have made a specific choice.

Believing there is a "perfect," "best," or "phenomenal" singular match is an overly simplistic view. Wanting that, looking for that, or expecting that is unrealistic and unreasonable.

———————

5

Is There an Alternative?

I'm so glad you asked.

People in relationships operate under two components: how they act in a relationship and the purpose the relationship serves for them. The way we act is fairly consistent from situation to situation; for example, a person who is assertive at work will likely be assertive at home. It is a part of who you are, based on how you were raised. That being said, people are complex and multidimensional. The way we act can be altered by our motivations or the purpose a relationship serves for us. In other words, we may act differently in different situations or for varying reasons.

The other people in the relationship also affect how a person acts or reacts.

For these reasons, personality tests which attempt to classify and categorize people have severe limitations. They all over-simplify reality.

The Patterns

I was in a long term relationship which suddenly ended. I was trying to figure out what had happened. My lover told me, quite bluntly, I was a "BTN." I shook my head, not understanding. A BT what? She said, "You know, Better Than Nothing!" Wow, that hurt!

In other words, I was just convenient at the time, someone to do things with. Of course, had I known that was my position with her at the time, I would have acted quite differently in the relationship. I would have invested less time, put in less effort, and spent less money. Had we both started with the same understanding of what the relationship was and what was expected, I could have made an informed choice or decision.

What I realized, after study, is people follow certain patterns when in relationships, whether business or personal: five major patterns dictate how we act and five minor patterns determine the purpose the relationship serves. How you act or react when faced with various situations or scenarios, as well as the purpose of the situation, sets the stage for the relationship.

There are reasons for the way we act. Much of the foundation for these patterns comes from our past, our upbringing, our social and economic perspective. For example, one study has found when people of different economic backgrounds were asked to estimate the physical size of a gold coin, the estimates were directly correlated to the person's economic station. That is, the lower a person's economic level, the larger the estimate of the physical size of the gold coin. We tend to over value, over estimate or over emphasize those things we desire but do not have.

Think about what you want in your various relationships. In business relationships, are you looking for someone to bounce ideas off of, or someone who includes you in their ideas, or someone to gossip with?

In friendships, are you looking for someone just to hang around with, someone to share a hobby with or someone for a small, specific part of your time?

In intimate relationships, are you looking for someone who is a pal or buddy or some of the intimacy without much of a bond or connection, "no strings attached"?

Then you are looking for a Convenience pattern relationship. Don't let the name fool you. The pattern of convenience or necessity is not necessarily casual or short lived. No matter the intensity or the length, all convenience relationships have some common characteristics: they're uncomplicated, they're easygoing, and they require little effort.

However, as Coach Stephanie McKenzie points out, "I've never really seen a convenience relationship work because usually one person knows it's convenience, and the other thinks it's something else." Been there done that!

In business relationships, are you looking for a creative thinker to balance your analytical, businesslike approach to solving problems, or possibly the other way around?

In friendships, are you looking for either someone to whom you can talk, share a bit of yourself or someone to whom you can listen, as they share themselves?

In intimate relationships, are you looking for someone who is a counter balance to you and you to them? Are you looking for someone who does the things you can do, but would rather not do, or someone who sees the things you do as valuable? Someone who enjoys balancing the checkbook, doing the cooking or vacuuming, or someone who appreciates that you do those things?

This Appreciation or Validation relationship pattern allows a person to shine in those specific areas or ways that make them feel most proud. A person's strengths or skills are specifically touted and valued. We each have our own special qualities that make us stand out, and we like being noticed for them.

For example, one man told me when it comes to vacations, his wife does all of the planning, and he just shows up. That is one of the things he really appreciates about her. This validates her as being the structured planner of the relationship.

In business relationships, are you looking for someone to follow or someone to lead?

In friendships, are you looking for consistency, people who can be counted on, or people who can count on you to act in certain predefined or predictable ways?

In intimate relationships, are you looking for a great deal of stability; do you need to know both what to expect of others and what is expected of you?

This relationship pattern is Scripted. The relationship follows a fairly clear, predefined and predictable format. Much like a movie, where you typically have one star surrounded by actors in supporting roles, everyone knows what to expect. The script may be set by societal norms or by media portrayals or by religious beliefs. All people need a certain amount of stability and consistency in their relationships; otherwise, it would be like being with a stranger. Every day would be trying, hectic. The differentiation is the degree of stability or consistency one needs. Contrary to popular belief, or mythology, it isn't just men who are the leaders or who are at the center of relationships; very often there is a strong wife or mother figure who binds, or holds a relationship, family, together.

For example, Coach Stephanie McKenzie says, "My dad was a 'Man's man.' He wanted a scripted, conventional relationship. He wanted a woman who would support him in his business, someone who had taken care of the organizing when he got home. With the scripted relationship, as with any relationship, everyone needs to know what role they play."

In business relationships, are you looking for an independent partner?

In friendships, are you looking for an equal, someone who's there most of the time, but not all of the time, someone who isn't clingy?

In intimate relationships, are you looking for someone you can share most anything with and they with you, and feel bonded, connected with, even though you spend time apart from one another?

Individual Assertion relationships are those which exhibit a pattern of a high degree of individualism while maintaining a strong bond to some home base. The participants in this type of relationship are connected in many, but not all, ways, and they focus on the shared interests while being free to pursue their own interests separately. The view in this type of relationship is we can't be, and don't even need to be, everything for each other.

In business relationships, are you looking for someone, or are you yourself someone, who doesn't toe the line or closely follow the same old process or procedures?

In friendships, are you looking for someone, or are you yourself someone, who keeps things fresh, has a unique and different outlook on life?

In intimate relationships, are you looking for someone, or are you yourself someone, who doesn't strictly adhere to the expectations of society?

This is an Acceptance relationship. We all want to be accepted for who we are. However, when you feel your views are unconventional or nontraditional, you don't want to be judged because of it. Acceptance is the ability to allow people to express themselves openly and honestly. Understand that acceptance is not agreement; it is the willingness to look past the inevitable differences and disagreements which will occur.

Let's face it, we all want to be accepted; however, most of us don't do things or act in such ways that are so out of the ordinary that acceptance is difficult or particularly special. In other words, for the most part, a certain amount of acceptance is routine; acceptance of the extraordinary is most valuable.

So to sum up the five major relationship patterns or how we act in relationships, let's look at them again:

- Convenience, Necessity
- Validation, Appreciation
- Scripted
- Individual Assertion
- Acceptance

Now let's look at the minor patterns, the types of relationships we search for.

In business relationships, are you looking for someone, or are you the type of person, who seems to make the day go by faster?

In friendships, are you looking for someone, or are you the type of person, who attends or participates in events, concerts, sports, movies, and so on?

In intimate relationships, are you looking for someone, or are you the type of person, who typically can find something to do or has something going on?

The Pastime pattern focuses on keeping busy in a fun and pleasant way. The purpose is to provide an escape from the humdrum, day to day, same old same old life.

In business relationships, are you looking for someone, or are you the type of person, who turns a negative into a positive? It may be a colleague who cheers you on when you feel like calling it quits.

In friendships, are you looking for someone, or are you the type of person, who provides moral support? It may be the person who listens patiently as you continue to ask "why."

In intimate relationships, are you looking for someone, or are you the type of person, who provides a shoulder to cry on? Perhaps it's connecting with someone who has had a similar experience, so they can relate and sympathize.

The Healing pattern provides support, specifically for those times when you or the other person must cope with some sort of loss or perceived failure. This pattern suggests a cleansing, therapeutic quality which facilitates moving past a difficult situation and moving forward in life.

By the way, it is typical to associate the Healing pattern with the commonly termed "rebound" relationship. But as Coach Stephanie McKenzie puts it, "You need to heal, not conceal. People hop from one relationship to another. I know of a person who is already off dating someone new when the ink isn't even dry on her divorce."

This is a case of transference; you have these pent up emotions needing to go someplace, so you use another person as a surrogate, either positively or negatively. One of those pieces of foolish and negative "common wisdom" is "If you want to get over one person, get under another one." As Mackenzie says, "I tell people that unless, and until, you have audited and identified the reasons for the demise of your last relationship, without snarling and blaming, you are not ready for your next relationship." In most cases, one hops from one relationship to another to avoid his or her own short comings as well as the grieving necessary at the end of a relationship. In other words, you aren't healing at all.

In addition, jumping from one relationship to another without any time either to heal or analyze and learn from the last situation almost ensures the missteps of the past will repeat themselves. As George Santayana said so wisely, "Those who cannot learn from history are doomed to repeat it." These replacement relationships have a high potential for the misuse or abuse of the emotions of the new third person.

Better advice might be to find a support system, friends, family or, if necessary, professional counseling. Review your previous relationship(s) and clearly define what could have and should have been done differently, at least those things within your own control. "Live, learn, love."

Walter Scott says it best in his nineteenth-century novel *The Bride of Lammermoor*: "It is best to be off wi' the old love before you're on wi' the new."

In business relationships, are you looking for someone, or are you the type of person, who promotes the acquiring of new skills, the pursuit of promotions?

In friendships, are you looking for someone, or are you the type of person, who inspires doing new, possibly unusual, things? Maybe it's eating sushi for the first time or enrolling in a Bollywood dance class.

In intimate relationships, are you looking for someone, or are you the type of person, who encourages personal, emotional, and intellectual growth?

The Experimental pattern offers a way to expand one's horizons in ways we might not otherwise have thought or been able to on our own.

In business relationships, are you looking for someone, or are you the type of person, who assists with getting settled into a new place or new routine?

In friendships, are you looking for someone, or are you the type of person, who welcomes others into or makes easy a foreign situation? It may be you who helps others merge or the other person who helps you.

In intimate relationships, are you looking for someone, or are you the type of person, who goes along for the journey either figuratively or literally?

Life is nothing if not ever-changing. From moving out of our parents' home, starting a new job, or getting married, we are perpetually in transition. Transitional patterns help us by offering someone who has either gone through it already or is willing to go through it with us.

In business relationships, are you looking for someone, or are you the type of person, who would rather do what you want to do, instead of what you need to do?

In friendships, are you looking for someone, or are you the type of person, who would rather play video games or go clubbing, instead of dealing with grocery shopping or paying the bills?

In intimate relationships, are you looking for someone, or are you the type of person, who would rather spend time away from home or family?

This pattern of Diversion or distraction allows people to take their minds off pressing or unpleasant issues, conflicts or confrontations. In fact, a rebound relationship follows the patterns of both Healing and Diversion.

Diversions are not always or necessarily negative. A person suffering from cancer, whose family and friends treat them very specially, may want a break to be seen and treated as a typical person.

For example, my sister had juvenile diabetes, now known as type 1 diabetes. As an adult, she would occasionally drink some wine, and this frustrated our mother. But my sister needed the occasional diversion. She needed to go out and have some fun, to be normal. It didn't mean she forgot the fact she was diabetic or that she was in any way self-destructive.

To sum up the five minor patterns in relationships:

- Pastime
- Healing
- Experimental
- Transitional
- Diversion

A leading cause of failed relationships is because the people in the relationship have different expectations; that is, they are in different patterns with different, or even cross, purposes. Of course, external forces may change a person's needs and, therefore, the purpose of a relationship.

For example, the death of a loved one launches the Healing and Transitional purposes of a relationship. In the case of the loss of a child, each person may deal with the tragedy differently, having different needs. If the parents cannot resolve how to heal, transition, and move forward together, their own relationship will be put into jeopardy. On the other hand, people may see themselves moving from friends to lovers, or from business associates to social friends, but the patterns we follow do not transform or progress from one to another. The patterns we follow are not interconnected in such a way that you inherently move from say "casual" to "accepting." The attributes of each pattern are independent and in some cases, contradictory. It is more along the lines of "You reap what you sow." You are very unlikely to get from a "pastime" friend to someone who is there to help you "heal." This is why it is so important to know what you want out of, and are willing to give into, the relationship because it isn't actually likely to magically change later. If you plant tomatoes, you mustn't be amazed that roses don't grow.

The point of this examination is to demonstrate the combination of the individuals and the ways in which they interact to determine how a relationship plays out its destination. You cannot get a specific type of relationship if the people involved don't add up to, or don't actually want,

Romeo and Juliet

Let's see how these patterns apply to Shakespeare's famous couple.

How did they act? They were looking for "strings;" therefore, Convenience wasn't it. They seemed to Appreciate and Validate each one's willingness to venture out on his/her own and brave new circumstances. Neither one was a clear leader or follower, so the Scripted pattern doesn't fit. They shared similarities in their situations; for example, their parents had definite plans for them which didn't take their own desires into account. Yet they were independent from their parents and from one another. Independent Assertion is a probability. Neither knew enough about the other, or themselves, to be truly Accepting.

What were the purposes of the relationship? They spent their free time together; however, that wasn't the primary reason for their relationship so Pastime isn't reasonable. Although they both survived tragedies in their lives, they didn't use their relationship to deal with those emotions, so Healing doesn't fit the bill. They did not consciously push one another to grow or Experiment. Both were moving from childhood to adulthood, and their families had plans for them, which would

Continued page 32

that type of relationship.

Now we have a destination, so we can prepare for the trip.

Continued from Page 31

have included things like more responsibilities. They faced similar Transitions, which they could share and empathize with. In effect, they used their relationship as a Diversion from what their families wanted. They could avoid the harsh reality of growing up by living in a fantasy of coupledom.

———————

(This chapter was informed by a typology devised by Carmen Lynch.)

6
CHAPTER

Why Do We Believe the Things We Do?

Ask yourself this question and the answers become obvious: because it's simple and easy to understand; it doesn't take any effort; it makes us feel good about ourselves by validating what we already believe about ourselves and others; and other people, especially people who we believe should know, believe it.

The economist John Kenneth Galbraith coined the term "conventional wisdom." We like to use that term to comfort ourselves, but for Galbraith, it had a negative connotation: "We associate truth with convenience, with what most closely accords with self-interest and personal well-being or promises best to avoid awkward effort or unwelcome dislocation of life. We also find highly acceptable what contributes most to self-esteem."

It must be simple, convenient, comforting, but what we believe is not necessarily true. If enough people say it is so, then it must be so, or so we think. If something is repeated often enough it is accepted by default, without question. There is a phenomenon in which even liars begin to believe their own lies if they repeat them often enough. This belief is akin to the idea that if you do something a certain number of times it becomes a habit; it becomes second nature; it is accepted with little or no thought.

Every new concept begins with a single individual. The group, the majority of people, doesn't even know about the concept, much less accept it. For example, at one point in time, the majority of people thought the earth was the center of the universe, until one person, Copernicus, said it wasn't. Others before him had speculated the very same thing; however, he wanted to prove it, one way or the other, and he wanted other people to understand it as well.

What I aim to do in this book is introduce you to and convince you regarding the evidence of how to interact with intimate partners, friends, and business acquaintances in ways you haven't even thought of. You're reading this book because the conventional wisdom hasn't worked for you. After all, why would you be looking for advice if you already knew what to do? The simple fact you need advice seems to put you at a disadvantage and at the mercy of others. You are here because you want good advice, a way to take control of your decision-making process.

7
CHAPTER

Why Do People Want Advice
in the First Place?

We desire advice because we would rather not learn how to fish! Anne Isabella Ritchie, a nineteenth-century novelist, said, "If you give a man a fish, he is hungry again in an hour; if you teach him to catch a fish, you do him a good turn."

People ask for advice because they either haven't been taught to think for themselves or they don't want to think for themselves. And although it's much easier to let others do the thinking for you because it carries less responsibility, it's also quite treacherous because it gives all of the control and power to others. When we ask for advice, we create a situation of reliance on others. The person who asks is forever asking, while the person advising is, essentially, a part of the relationship.

We attend school in order to learn how to think and answer questions for ourselves, without the need to constantly ask others. Endeavors such as reading, writing, and mathematics are significant, to be sure; however, long before these even come into play, and even more necessary to survival, are relationship skills. We will spend from four to eight years in high school and college learning these operations, while devoting a very small amount of time learning about, or attempting to understand, relationships. We should spend at least the same amount of time and effort learning about relationships as we spend on our schooling, our jobs, our hobbies, or our entertainment.

Think about it: if you ask someone for advice, you are taking his perspective, his rationale, his ideas as your own, ideas which may not fit your situation or your values. In Cat Stevens' song "Father and Son," in which the father tries to give the son advice, the son sings the line "If they were right I'd agree, but it's them they know not me." Even though the father's advice is good and sound, it's from his perspective, not the son's. One knows one's own situation and values and lifestyle. The advisor does not.

If all we did was what others told us to do, how would we learn, how would we experience anything new, how would we develop?

Learning to fish, and deal with relationships, requires, time, effort, and sacrifice.

Of course, people cannot learn entirely on their own; they need either to be taught or to actively seek out answers. However, they need to understand the "why" behind the answers, and they have to be able to think critically, using proper decision-making techniques and processes in order to assess what they are being taught. If you don't know the "why" you run the risk of, at best, simply wasting your time and effort on something that doesn't apply to you or, at worst, being taken advantage of.

Bad advice is like old fish, it isn't worth consuming, and it can make you sick.

8

How Does Bad Advice Get Perpetrated?

Bad or incorrect or inaccurate advice is everywhere, from sources such as books, movies and the internet, and from people such as family, friends and even experts. "Conventional wisdom" in the way Galbraith meant it is generated for a few basic reasons.

First, it is an over simplification of the underlying information. Einstein has been paraphrased as saying, "Everything should be made as simple as possible, but no simpler." We generally like things to be kept simple, but the problem is with each iteration of simplification, some of the meaning and, therefore, value is lost. At some point of simplification, the advice doesn't accurately represent or convey the original message. For example, you've heard these phrases: "Buy low and sell high" and "relationships require communication." When you think about it, these are vague, obvious, and inane. If you didn't already know either of these gems, then you shouldn't be at a place where you need them. You shouldn't be in the business of buying or selling or looking for—much less being in a relationship. Gross over-simplification has rendered these well-intentioned pieces of advice utterly meaningless.

Second is misunderstanding the core concept and, therefore, asking the wrong question(s), looking for the wrong cause. When we ignore the underlying motivations, focusing only on the outcome or result, we come to incorrect conclusions. Remember those personality models, the Big Five and the Myers Briggs Temperament Index? They focus on the actions not the reasons for or behind those actions. In fact, I have found that opposites manifest themselves in identical ways.

For example, I have a buddy, Lale, a fairly average man in many regards, average height, a bit stout, unassuming, mustachioed, who grew up self-conscious about his crooked teeth and, therefore, his smile. (Notice the mustache.) As a child and throughout his adolescence and young adulthood, he wouldn't smile at people because he was unhappy with the appearance of his teeth. Then he discovered braces in his late-twenties, rectified what he considered to be the problem, and began to smile at everyone.

Some people told him because he hadn't smiled, they thought he was cold, distant, and arrogant. In fact, he was quite the opposite; he was a nice, even shy, guy who was embarrassed by the way he saw himself. So, in this case, opposite feelings manifested themselves in identical outcomes. He wouldn't smile because he was shy, but others thought he was the opposite of shy, arrogant.

We have all heard "Don't judge a book by its cover" and "Things are rarely as they appear," but do you know how, where, or when, to apply those maxims? Even if you may think the picture is not quite clear, does it ever cross your mind the picture is actually the very opposite? Unfortunately, people often assume the worst, not the best of others. Anais Nin has wisely said, "We don't see things as they are, we see them as we are." When you see someone crying, do you think tears of sorrow or tears of joy? When you hear someone raise his voice, do you think exuberance or anger? So someone thinks if I don't smile at him, it is because I don't like him; therefore, his not smiling must be for the same reason. I have trouble believing he might be embarrassed because that is not how I feel. What we see or perceive is a reflection of ourselves. Henry David Thoreau said, "It's not what you look at that matters, it's what you see."

Another example of opposites looking the same: people think "venting" is a good way to reduce stress and prevent lashing out at others, an idea going back to Aristotle, who thought you needed to release pent-up energy or fluids (crying or sex). Freud made the idea part of his psychology. However, in the 1990s, Brad Bushman studied whether or not venting actually worked. He found those who vented were more violent towards others. Venting, yelling or screaming, raises hormones such as adrenaline and allows a person to dwell on the offending person or incident whereas simply taking deep breaths, relaxing and finding distractions will have potentially calming effects. We think venting will keep us from hurting ourselves and others, but it does the opposite.

People judge, assume, or conclude based on the act they perceive without knowing the underlying cause or motivations of the act.

A third reason people generate and trust bad advice is they misinterpret the data, thereby coming up with a wrong answer or finding the wrong effect. For example, most of us believe a person is either "right-brained" or "left-brained" and each side of the brain holds specific strengths and corresponds to personality traits. There are books and seminars dedicated to teaching people how to train the "weaker" side of the brain to develop creative or analytical skill, including *Drawing on the Right Side of the Brain* which sold over 2.5 million copies.

This concept, however, is a misinterpretation of the data. Neuroscience demonstrates the different sides of the brain exhibit certain strengths for certain tasks. However, the two sides of the brain work together, and there is no evidence you can train one side. Simply on an intuitive level, think about it: if we could train or retrain the various areas of the brain, then any loss of functionality on one side—due to an accident or birth malformation—could just be transferred to another part of the brain.

Bad advice is also brought about because of a reversal of what is thought to be the cause and the effect.

There was a tribe which noticed healthy people had more lice than did the unhealthy. Their conclusion? Lice make a person healthy. Of course, the truth is healthy people are a better host and, therefore, the lice are able to increase their population. Lice don't make a person healthy.

What is Bias?

Bad advice comes from bias or a tendency to see things a certain way, sometimes called a prejudice ("prejudice" means to "pre-judge," to make judgments without first gathering the relevant, pertinent information) and is often unreasoned. Every person has biases of some kind or another, intentional or unintentional which begin in childhood, when we were unquestioning, trusting, naive, and unaware of the complexities of the world around us. An example of a childhood-generated bias could be as simple as preferring one type of bread over another because our parents said it was better for us. These biases often continue into adulthood unabated and may toughen depending on what or who we trust or question. So even scientists, judges, and mathematicians—those we expect to be free of biases so they can make trustworthy decisions—have the potential and the impulse to be biased. Bias is a natural phenomenon, one requiring a great deal of effort to overcome because it is rooted in our socioeconomic upbringing and continuing circumstances. Even though we may become fully aware of the potential for bias and the harmful effects biases can create, we are either too lazy or too fearful to confront them.

One form of bias stems from "over exposure." A person who is placed in a unique situation tends to view that set of circumstances as the norm rather than the exception. Doctors tend to overestimate the occurrences of the specific diseases they study and by which they are surrounded. Law enforcement officers tend to overestimate incidences of crime and may, therefore, view every citizen as a potential criminal.

So from decision-making to taking advice, many aspects of human behavior are studied and understood, but both as individuals and as a society, we continually ignore the findings. In other words, we don't apply what we already know about human behavior to ourselves or others. We don't question our actions or motivations though we may question the actions or motivations of others without serious understanding.

We are often willing to take the advice of experts, for example, but the title "expert" is not technical in nature; it is not rewarded or earned. What makes a person an "expert"? What standards do they follow, and to whom have they demonstrated their abilities? It's important to remember or acknowledge even the so-called experts have human biases, past baggage, human behaviors and traits which have the potential to affect their judgments and conclusions.

Advertising is brilliant at creating conventional wisdom. Listerine was developed in the late-nineteenth century as a powerful surgical antiseptic, but it didn't catch on with the general public until the 1920s when it was pitched as a solution for "chronic halitosis." Until their advertising campaign, bad breath was not considered a devastating condition. Even the very word "halitosis" was coined by the company. Listerine did not make mouthwash a product so much as it made "halitosis" a problem.

Even the crime crackdown in New York City in the 1990s is an example of how "advertising" can present a conclusion which is a misinterpretation of the data. Mayor Giuliani and the police chief began cracking down on incidental crimes using the theory that major crimes like homicides would decline. The crime rate did drop and they got a lot of credit for it, but the rate had begun to drop earlier and the crackdown was responsible for a miniscule amount. Do I need to tell you they took full credit for the outcome?

Statistics are one way experts convince us of certain "facts" from which we conclude advice. I was watching a talk show one day on which the guest, a Ph.D., had collected a number of statistics and then written a book on what men and women prefer in relationships. One statistic indicated people prefer a certain genre of music over others while having sex. The host promptly asked where her preferred genre of music ranked; to her shock, she was informed it wasn't even one of the categories in the study. In effect, the "expert" had done nothing more than collect data on his own personal preferences, which could be categorized as that of a white male in his mid-forties. His conclusions were certainly not representative of society in general. They were biased.

Another form of bias is misinformation, sometimes deliberate and sometimes unintentional. An example of deliberate misinformation is demonstrated in one study which asked women about the number of sex partners they had. The study used three different methods to gather the information. First, women were asked simply to answer a questionnaire while an administrator waited outside the room. The second step was to ask women to complete a questionnaire while an administrator was present in the room. Lastly, women were asked to answer a questionnaire while they were monitored by a lie detector. The results were telling: the number of reported sex partners increased as the chance of being caught lying increased. In other words, people lie even with the veil of anonymity. This study alone should cause us to question the findings of the self-report style surveys.

Sometimes bias is demonstrated in relaying unintentional misinformation. This can be driven by what people want to happen rather than what actually does happen, a "do as I say not as I do" mentality. Have you ever known someone who doesn't take his or her own advice? These instances range from people who tell you not to stay in a bad relationship even though they find excuses to stay in their own bad relationship to people who tell you to take more risks while they sit quietly at home watching television or playing on the computer.

Of course, people are known to "change their minds," but it is more along the lines of saying one thing and doing another. But why?

One reason for this dichotomy is we can't know all of the various criteria which will come into play in reality. It is easy enough to say this is the way you will act in a certain situation; however, when it comes right down to it, faced with having to deal with the many possibilities, what we decide may be very different and still be completely justified.

When I was sixteen, I heard about a friend of the family whose wife had cheated on him. He was having trouble deciding what to do: leave, stay, or something in between. At the time, I plainly stated if that were ever to happen to me, the relationship would be over. Who knew that just nine years later I would be faced with the very same decision? I could not have known at the age of sixteen the great difference my having a four-year-old daughter would have on the difficulty of the decision. It wasn't that I had changed my mind; instead, the question, the circumstances, had changed. The problem, life, isn't exactly as we expect it to be.

It is easy to make grand statements when we don't actually believe we will be held to them. I had heard of a study that claimed ninety percent of women claimed they would leave their families, husbands, children, and home if they were given ten million dollars. I sincerely doubt if that ever came to fruition so many women would act on it.

The fact is we don't know ourselves as well as we think we do. In truth, we can't see the future; therefore, we can't see ourselves in that future. In addition, our motives, the underlying reasons we act in a certain way, may be different in *similar* situations. We've all heard of people who act out of what was considered their normal behavior, but often that behavior is based on extenuating circumstances. Sometimes we act in the heat of the moment, which leads to such things as guilt or buyer's remorse. People say or do something in a rash manner, without thinking it through, and then regret it afterwards.

In all of these cases, the advice "Be careful what you wish for" is apropos.

Based on these conclusions of human behavior, it is clear self-report studies cannot account for actions as accurately as they suggest. For example, research shows women consistently report they would prefer to have an intimate relationship with or date someone with whom they were friends. However, when shown pictures of friends and strangers they, by measurement, are consistently more aroused by strangers.

In another study, researchers created two groups, one of single people and the other of couples in a relationship. The two groups were shown pictures of other couples at various stages and in various situations within their relationships. When asked to comment on the state of the relationships of the couples in the pictures, the couples fared worse than the singles. This, of course, is contrary to expectations, because we assume people in a relationship know about relationships. The results suggest people who are in a relationship are so focused and biased by their single relationship and their own partner they are out of touch with relationships in general.

The moral here is don't blindly assume people who are in a relationship are good sources of advice.

Many personality tests require people give their own opinion of themselves, but this is your biased view which may or may not be accurate. Stereotypical biases, such as race, nationality, and gender all come into play. People don't know their true selves with a great degree of confidence which should cause us to question the findings of the self-report style studies.

Statistics don't lie, but the people who use them definitely do.

———•◦•———

9

How Bad Advice Makes the Rounds

I once was invited to be on a panel for a seminar on relationships where we, the panel of people with varying expertise, were answering questions about relationships and giving advice to the attendees. An audience member asked how far one should go to hold on to a relationship. One of the panelists responded with a story of a woman who, after suffering physical abuse at the hands of her mate, remained in the relationship until her abuser realized the error of his ways and changed for the better. The clear implication was sometimes you have to suffer to love.

Of course, this is extremely bad advice and results from an incorrect decision-making process.

Herodotus, a philosopher of the sixth century BCE, said, "A decision is wise, even though it leads to disastrous consequences if the evidence at hand indicated that it was the best one to make; and a decision is foolish, even though it leads to the happiest possible consequences, if it is unreasonable to expect those consequences." For example, every day, all around the world, people drive home after a night of drinking. They wake up the next morning in their own beds. Not having had an accident and not having hurt themselves or anyone else, they think they made good, correct decisions. Nothing could be further from the truth. People shouldn't drive when they're drunk. Regardless of the good outcome, this is a bad decision. These people used the outcome to justify their actions.

When outcome is used as a means for decision-making, we are capable of doing anything and hurting anyone in the process.

The Ends Justify the Means

Mr. Spock, of Star Trek fame, was fond of saying, "The needs of the many outweigh the needs of the few." Not too distant from this aphorism is the common saying, "Sacrifice the few for the needs of the many," a quotation from Charles Dickens' Tale of Two Cities, and fitting for everything from office politics and government regulations to the death penalty and genocide. But let's look at the implications of this idea often used as an attempt to excuse "the ends justify the means." Seeing only the outcome instead of using the proper, relevant information suggests a poor decision-making process, irrational and illogical. (Sorry, Mr. Spock.)

During the U.S. war for independence, fewer revolutionaries fought than British soldiers. Using the "logic" of sacrificing the few, the revolutionaries should have been killed to save the British. During World War II, approximately six million Jews were murdered, but during that same time over twenty million Russians alone were killed. Accounting for all military and civilians from various countries, over thirty mil-

Continued Page 47

My soon-to-be ex-wife took the stand when I was in court for my divorce / custody case. In an effort to discredit me, she painted a picture of me as a cruel, emotionless, even abusive tyrant. In her exuberance to malign my character, she claimed I had always been this type of vile individual, and I was never anything other than that. My lawyer asked her, "If he had always been this sort of person, why then did you marry him?" Her answer was "for the finances." She explained that at the time she was living with her parents and she wanted to get out of their house. Because I had a good job, I could afford to pay for the things she wanted. For her, the ends, getting out of her parents' home and having finances at her disposal, justified the means, marrying and using a person she clearly despised, namely, me.

If all we are concerned with is the end, that is the outcome, to what lengths are we willing to go to achieve that end? Is lying, cheating, stealing, abuse, harm, or even murder acceptable? And what about when this is used not by you, but against you?

When a new medicine is produced, it must go through rigorous testing, in many cases for years, before the general public is exposed to it. Medicine is vetted using trusted procedures, using trusted processes and manufactured by trusted sources. Even with exhaustive testing, there have been medicines which either didn't work as promised or were actually harmful.

Just as with bad medicine, bad advice either doesn't work as promised or expected or, worse, it can be harmful, actually damaging your relationship.

Continued from Page 46

lion people were killed, not including the Jews. Using the rationale of "sacrifice the few to save the many," the war should not have been fought.

Imagine a group of one hundred people made up of convicted felons, murders, rapists, and pedophiles, and a group of ten people consisting of four cancer researchers, three Noble peace prize winners, and three school teachers. Clearly, the few are of a greater value than the many.

Why in the world would we kill the few in order to save the many? It has nothing to do with the number of people and everything to do with the ideals, the values, the facts, and, of course, the characteristics of the people.

Once a bit of bad advice or incorrect "conventional" wis-dom is released into the wild, it spreads like a virus. It cannot be contained and is passed from person to person, generation to generation until society becomes infected.

Medicine comes with warnings and conditions: "Don't operate heavy equipment," "Take with a meal," warnings designed to protect you from the most harmful effects. Unfortunately, advice rarely comes with warnings or conditions. How often have you heard a recall on advice? How often have you heard, "This is bad advice, incorrect or incomplete conventional wisdom?" "If you do this it will be detrimental, harmful, or damaging, to you and or your relationship." Instead, it is stated as absolute, applying to all people and all situations: "Stick with your partner," "Love her/him more than yourself," "Sacrifice for the relationship." Bad medicine can ruin your health or your life; bad advice can ruin your relationships, which in turn can ruin your health or your life. So who is the trusted source who verifies the advice and conventional wisdom you use?

Addiction

It's worth noting that when we are in an intimate relationship our body chemistry changes, producing different quantities of hormones. This is akin to being on drugs. Just like being on drugs, ending a relationship cold turkey causes us to go through a withdrawal of sorts. Replacing one person with another is simply replacing one addiction or drug with another.

Often, bad advice gets spread and solidified in society as sayings, phrases, proverbs, or sound bites. Here are a few examples of advice often given to people about their relationships and, of course, the reasons *why* you should not believe in them or take the action suggested.

Trust Your First Instinct

This piece of folk wisdom is often applied to multiple choice tests, but it can also be applied to dating. Students are often told the first choice is usually the correct one and changing their answer usually won't result in a higher score. But research has proven the opposite is correct. More than sixty studies have concluded when students change an answer on a multiple choice test, they are more likely to change it from a wrong answer to a right one.

When in doubt, we're usually wise not to trust our first instincts. Our first hunches are only hunches, and if we have reason to doubt them, then we should reconsider, think it through. If, after proper consideration, we find a better choice, take it. Think about this: Where do first impressions come from? Are they as "first" as we believe them to be? From birth, we are bombarded with sights, sounds, smells, touches, and tastes. We relate, connect and correlate these experiences to everything we do for the rest of our lives. After about the age of five, there are very few truly new, unique firsts. We use all these past experiences to interpret our present circumstances and situations. In other words, our "firsts" are anything but.

The term "imprinting" was coined in studies with animals. Naturalist Konrad Lorenz discovered the actuality of it when goslings became connected to him because he was the first thing they saw upon hatching. A similar phenomenon has been observed in studies with humans. People have a tendency to become anchored to their first impressions. So when something new comes along, people may change from one impression to another by relating the new item with an even stronger previous experience, circumstance or pattern.

Better advice might be "Think it through" or "Look before you leap." You get the idea; stop, if only for a few seconds, and make an actual (informed) decision before going through with your actions.

All's Fair in Love and War

As early as World War I, it was decided the use of chemical weapons was cruel and unusual. (Of course we could debate how one form of killing is less cruel than any other, but we'll leave that for a different discussion.) People decided the use of certain forms of warfare were not acceptable. Basically, it was agreed if "you" don't this to "us" then "we" won't do the same thing to "you." World War II saw the wide spread inclusion of civilians in the aggression. Actions such as raping women, certain forms of torture, and mass extinctions are decidedly not acceptable, reasonable, or "fair." It was decided that certain acts, such as genocide, were actually crimes, War Crimes. If all is fair in war, then these rationalizations simply cannot be justified.

Now let's look at Love. Most people would agree deeds such as killing your rival, cheating on your partner, physical abuse, or enslavement are not acceptable although people do all those things and more in the name of Love.

There are many behaviors, in both Love and War, which are clearly not acceptable or "fair." The phrase "All's Fair in Love and War" is either a misunderstanding of the core concept, what is love and what is war, or it is simply intentionally flippant.

This little bit of advice is used as an excuse for bad behavior.

Applying this flippancy to a real war or to an actual relationship is, in fact, dangerous. Better advice might be to do all you reasonably can and put forth your best effort while not intentionally or maliciously spreading harm to yourself or others.

Absence Makes the Heart Grow Fonder versus Out of Sight Out of Mind

These two common sayings advise opposite reactions to the same behavior. Mutually exclusive, they can't both be correct. The question, then, is which one is the correct behavior?

Actually, both ways of reacting are incorrect because the perspective is from the idea that the situation is what drives the fondness.

This is a case of the reversal of cause and effect.

When you reverse the perspective, it's easier to understand the idea that regardless of whether you are near to or far from the one you are connected to, your feelings will not change or wane. Regardless of distance, if your feelings are not strong, your relationship can't flourish or even survive.

The Heart Wants What the Heart Wants

This bit of conventional wisdom defies logic. The head, not the heart, can "want," can formulate thoughts which become desires. The heart deals in the emotional.

The main difficulty with this advice is it permits, even encourages, you to let emotions control you regardless of whether it is good for you or others. As it is your wants—and not your needs—there are no limits or boundaries. Like the advice "All's fair in love and war," this piece of wisdom can be used to justify any and all actions: cheating, pedophilia, you name it. It's all in the name of love because you can't control yourself.

From time to time, don't we all want "to have our cake and eat it, too"? Just as the advice "If it feels good, do it" is selfish, this advice shows a disregard for the feelings of those around you. What if what feels good to you causes harm to you or to someone else? Should you still do it? Obviously not. This is a sign of immaturity. This is another example of bad advice justifying bad behavior, which is an intentional bias towards personal dysfunction.

Now saying "Never follow your heart" or "Never do what feels good" is no better than saying "Always follow your heart." These are extreme, and therefore untenable, goals. You can still appease the heart or do what feels good so long as you are mindful of how others are affected as well as the consequences to yourself. The mind provides the restraint. There has to be a balance, a combination of both heart and mind; this is what we call good judgment.

Better advice might be to balance your desires of the heart with the temperaments of the mind; don't be either excessively controlled or uncontrolled. "Look before you leap."

You Get What You Give

This advice sounds like a guarantee, but "there are no guarantees." On the one hand, this piece of wisdom implies there is no risk, which may sound good; however, there is equally no reward, or gain, which isn't good. If there is risk and it is good and there is gain and it is good, then there would be no reason for making this statement as everyone would be acting in accordance with it already: giving and getting equally. Even if it were the case that each was giving and getting equally, because there are at least two people involved in any type of transaction, and since you don't have control over other people's actions or reactions, this situation simply cannot be possible. People do not act in accordance with complete and exact reciprocity. You may give more than you receive in return or vice versa.

Also, notice this statement is strictly from the perspective of the giver; from the perspective of the receiver he or she is getting more than giving, at least originally, which immediately proves this statement impossible.

What does it even mean to "get what you give"? There are many ways to interpret this piece of advice. One is through the concept of charity, giving without the expectation of getting anything in return. That notion may set up an attitude of entitlement or expectation on the part of the receiver where none exists. However, continuing to give more in the hopes of getting something in return can have the effect of reinforcing bad behavior. People will come to expect more from you without being required to do anything in return. You may be taken for granted and or taken advantage of. The idea of equality is not easily quantified. First, is equality truly identical? If I supply you with ten dollars, should I expect ten dollars in return, literally? This would make any sort of shopping a total waste of time. Second, what about the time component? Should you not expect any sort of interest if a long enough time passes?

So how might this wisdom play out in relationships? What might be the ramifications? We need to give in increments, small doses, and be mindful of what we are getting in return. Would you loan a stranger ten thousand dollars, one thousand dollars, a hundred dollars? No. Banks don't operate this way and neither should you. People have to build up credit (trust), slowly, measured, and metered, over a period of time.

So you have to give a little, get a little in return, and give a little more. Ramp it up over time, keeping an eye on the returns. If you don't receive in return that which you feel you deserve, then reevaluate your giving.

That is self-respect, self-worth.

This advice is a case of wishful thinking. We would like to believe that if we give, we should be rewarded. However, the reality of this exchange demonstrates that outcome is clearly not the case.

10

Bad Dating Advice

You know some of this advice if you think about it. It's what people say to you when you mention you're having trouble finding someone special. It's the "conventional wisdom" that everyone parrots. Here are some examples and why they don't work; they're not going to help you date successfully.

Try Something New to Find Someone to Date

If you're having difficulty finding people to date, try something new and put yourself out there. There are a number of flaws in this nugget of advice.

First, this isn't who you are. If you try skydiving and you happen to meet someone with whom you click, you may be in for a shock. This may be a major part of who they are, their lifestyle. You are experimenting with who you are, but the skydiver already knows who she is. She wants to skydive.

What happens when after say six months, you've had your fill of this activity, and you want to try something new? In contrast, the person you have connected with is entirely happy with this activity.

If you try to convince the other person not to skydive and instead to ice skate, this action will come across as trying to change her.

Second, people find confidence appealing. Confidence comes with comfort and experience. But doing things you aren't comfortable with, or experienced at, makes you less confident and, therefore, less appealing.

Better advice would be to do things you already like to do, and find others who like what you do. When you are experimenting with new things remember you are just a tourist, just passing through. Relationships should either be avoided until you are sure you're staying or entered into with caution and the understanding of the tenuous nature.

Date Many People at Once — Increase Your Odds

There are many situations in which we can show that doing something a great number of times will yield all possible results. The thought in this piece of advice is if we date everyone, we are bound to find the best possible match.

There is a certain impracticality of dating everyone though. Even dating a large number of people will take its toll on people's emotions as well as their time and their finances.

First, you'll have started all your relationships with the perspective of them not being exclusive, significant, or intense, so you won't be invested in, or alert to, any one of your relationships. If you aren't putting any great or special effort into any one of your relationships, then why would you choose one over another? Why would any of the other people choose you?

Second, you'll be judging each person against the others. Since no one person is likely to have all of the qualities you seek, how will you choose or differentiate one from another? It's more probable you will use the differences against each person, thereby eliminating all of them rather than choosing one of them.

In effect, these aren't significant relationships: "A friend to everyone is a friend to no one." If the relationship works the way it is, it is simply because of the type of relationship it is, that is non-exclusive. What would happen if you want to become exclusive with one person, but he or she is either happy the way things are or wants to end the current relationship?

This conventional wisdom to "play the field" is not socially or behaviorally sound for finding a singular relationship. You are setting yourself up for failure.

Better advice might be that it's all right to have multiple relationships so long as you keep in mind this method is not to be used for narrowing down or finding "the one," a singular relationship. If what you want is a singular relationship, then you must be in that type of relationship from the start. Don't expect, in return, what you yourself are not willing to give. "You reap what you sow."

So Many Friends!

It is important to recognize that given the number of hours in a day and the level of interaction we need to maintain a connection, we can have only a limited number of friends. In fact, there is an estimate of the number of connections we can have at any given time. Titled the Dunbar number, after the person who did the calculation, you can keep up with about 150 people at once.

Play Hard to Get

People often give the advice to "play hard to get," but research suggests men are less interested in women who are "standoffish" than women who are receptive to their advances. This advice shows up in other situations that we will encounter later, so I will come back to it; just know it is there and look for it.

11
CHAPTER

Where Does "Conventional Wisdom" Come From?

My attempts here to analyze "conventional wisdom" logically are to show when we don't question the information or the motivation behind it, we open ourselves to be victims of such bad advice, incorrect conventional wisdom, or junk science. There is a saying, "An empty barrel makes the most noise," meaning the people who know the least say the most, and they do so loudly or vigorously. These loud, and sometimes prolific, people resort to tactics of force, aggression, or simply overwhelming any opposing beliefs rather than being rational, being able to justify, or even to explain their positions.

Throughout history, those people who have had either the most time for, or the most access to, the prevailing media have used it to their own advantage, whatever the topic.

In previous centuries, that group was only the privileged few. They were the educated and the only ones able to convey, and make permanent through writings, their own thoughts or feelings on a subject. Therefore, much of what we think we know, and take for granted, from earlier times comes not from the common man but rather from the uncommon ones, the rare few. Put another way, the anecdotes, advice, and conventional wisdom come from the minority, not the majority.

The minority are those who have some stake in the matter; they have the most problems or concerns or dysfunctions and, therefore, have some of the greatest motivations to involve and immerse themselves in their respective fields. The most powerful motivators are fear, loss, and longing.

Some bits of advice or conventional wisdom describe not what is known about a topic but what is wished for, the desired outcome. A person may have wished for a different outcome and, therefore, claim that is the correct, and only, acceptable outcome. My advice: "Be careful what you wish for!"

———◆◆———

12
CHAPTER

Stories and Jokes of Morality and Ethics

These are further instances of "bad advice" and false "conventional wisdom" and how they permeate into culture. For example, I recently saw a preview for a female comic doing her stand-up routine; her shtick was bashing the loyalty of men. She is a well-known lesbian, so just what exactly does she know regarding men in relationships? It is just this type of pandering to the accepted stereotypes of the convention that tends to solidify the myths of the gender differences.

Everyone laughs when comedians bash the genders—more so when it is not their own—but little do people realize they begin to believe these ridiculous jokes represent the majority rather than the minority, an isolated or misrepresented incident.

From time to time, people create stories, fables, as morality or ethical tales. Of course, sometimes they just want to make a joke and see how far it will go, how gullible others are. However, no disclaimer accompanies these tales to notify the reader or listener these stories are fiction, fantasy, fairy tales, not fact and not to be taken literally.

For example, the Oprah Winfrey book club was well known for its picks and pans. Any author making it onto the recommended reading list was sure to get notoriety. At one point, Oprah recommended an autobiography dealing with drug addiction and recovery. It related trials and tribulations the sympathetic author had dealt with and, as with all good books, ended on the happy note of his return from purgatory and redemption.

Oprah widely praised the book and the author. However, people later discovered the book was an exaggeration, to say the least. But even after that revelation, Oprah's stance was that due to the uplifting message, the book was still valuable and worthy of praise. At some point, she reconsidered and realized the damage these false stories actually impart. She withdrew her praise.

In this case, the trivialization of the plight of those who actually suffer the affliction, the misinformation that others cannot practically put to use, and the false hope the book offered were detrimental to those who read it. The message resounds: if you cannot achieve what this person achieved, then there must be something wrong with you. But he had never achieved what he claimed.

A concept widely applied to politics, relationships, and economics is "The few are the cause of the many." The things we believe to be normal may actually be those which are exaggerated or blown out of proportion. For example, we know the majority of complaints in any business are due to a small set of issues just as a majority of a company's income is typically due to a few large customers. ("The squeaky wheel gets the grease," we like to say.) This is formalized in mathematics as the Pareto Principle, also known as "the 80-20 Rule of Thumb."

By analogy, we can surmise the majority of advice, or observations and perceptions of society, come from a minority of people or a very few actual social occurrences. Studies have shown it can take as little as five percent of people to influence a group. If that minority does not have the best interest of the group (society) at heart, only their views will be seen and their interests served.

In the modern world, almost anyone with a computer has the ability to publish and publicize his or her own personal thoughts. Although this may seem an improvement over the former centuries when a select few had the ability to get their ideas into the public forum—the common man now has a voice—in fact, many individuals are self-serving and driven by personal motives; therefore, their thoughts are theirs alone and not representative of society in general. Their advice, likewise, is often self-serving and does not truly describe the conditions of the many.

Studies show people who voice their opinions in person, online, or otherwise, are those people who are polarized, either positively or negatively. Polar opposites are extremists and, therefore, not representative of the majority, which typically has a more moderate combination of beliefs and falls somewhere in the middle of an issue.

Studies of online comments indicate the wide extent of effects of negative or incorrect comments on the beliefs of the majority. *Popular Science*, reacting to negative or incorrect comments and citing a study led by University of Wisconsin-Madison professor Dominique Brossard, has gone so far as to disable the ability to comment on their online articles. *Christianity Today* also ended online comments on its news and features, and the news service Reuters pulled the plug on its comment page for news stories.

Another study, titled "The Dark Triad of Personality," showed strong positive correlations between commenting frequency, trolling enjoyment, troll identity and sadism, psychopathy, and Machiavellianism.

Clearly, the minority isn't the appropriate source for the average person (the majority) for advice on anything; the minority is the exception and not the rule.

Who is right? The "conventions" or the scientific research? Because there is so much bad and incorrect advice in the marketplace, it isn't enough to simply focus on what "to do;" we also need to know what "not to do." We need different, even unconventional, advice in order to make a change.

———•◦•———

13
CHAPTER

My Persona Model

The amount and intensity of preparation for your journey depends on the destination. Going down to the local store certainly doesn't require the same amount of preparation and intensity as climbing Mount Kilimanjaro. In the same way, a temporary, short term, shallow relationship doesn't require the same degree of preparation as does a long term, intense, deeply connected relationship. The most efficient way to get to a destination is to plan your journey and pack accordingly.

If you don't prepare, you can expect a rough journey.

There are two parts to preparation: packing our bags and knowing what to pack. We've all heard people carry baggage into their relationships. "Baggage" itself is not negative although it has amassed that incorrect connotation. Your baggage represents who you are and where you've been, both positively and negatively. If you think about it, our yesterdays prepare us for our tomorrows.

In your past, you may have encountered a specific situation which seems always to end in one way, whether good or bad. You've come to believe, and even expect, this is the only way this situation can end. Another person may never have encountered that situation or they may be open-minded, which you see as naïve. Other people may have had the same or similar situations which ended in a number of different ways. They may not be quite as certain as you are.

Inside of your baggage you will pack whatever you believe you will need for your future based on your past. For example, you know if you are going to a tropical island, you'll need a bathing suit, shorts, and loose fitting tops. If you're going to Kilimanjaro, you'll need quite different supplies and clothing.

So what you pack in your baggage is important, but the biggest concern is how we deal with, or carry, our baggage. We might even say people who check their bags are able to separate themselves from their past, at least for periods of time, whereas, people who carry on their bags cannot let go of the past. Those who carry their bags with them wherever they go aren't able to put aside what has happened, their beliefs and expectations, in order to see what is happening now or what might happen in the future.

Of course, sometimes it isn't so much what's in your bag as your being unrealistic or unreasonable about the good or the bad, being overly optimistic or pessimistic. If we focus too heavily on the past while not placing enough value on the present, we maintain our hindsight bias. That only takes us into the past, not forward into the future.

We need to learn why we carry the bags we do. We need to figure out what to pack in the bags and *how* to carry them. I want to present a persona model answering those questions.

Unfortunately, existing personality models, like the Big Five and the Myers Briggs Temperament Index, do not accurately represent what we know about people and human behavior because these models strictly describe the outward manifestation of how people express themselves. They do not take into account *why* people might choose to express themselves the way they do, or in which situations they might choose to express themselves differently.

If you have taken some personality tests, you'll find some of the questions difficult to answer as I did. It can be like reading a horoscope, where the wording is so vague there is more than one possible, true, answer. For example, "If you were a tree, what kind of tree would you be?" I always want to respond, "Trees can't read or write, so I can't possibly answer that question now!"

My Persona Model takes into account, and encompasses, the reasons and rationale of why we do the things we do, as well as how we act in different situations. Our reasoning for doing the things we do, and how different situations affect how we act, is ingrained into us from childhood, through means such as selective exposure, social and economic bias, and interaction with others.

But first, we have to know the players.

———•◆•———

14
CHAPTER

Getting to Know People, Starting with You

I n any relationship—business, social, family, friendship or intimate—
we need to get to know the players. In business, it begins with the
interview process, in friendships it is simple observation, for intimate
relationships we need both. We need to know what questions to ask and
how to interpret the responses.

In researching this book, I talked to a woman who occasionally
coaches other women how to interact with men. Confident and well-
spoken, she is a slender, pale-skinned woman who wears her wavy blonde
hair just past her shoulders. She related this story: She took two women
who wanted coaching to a local watering hole. They identified a number
of potentially interesting men hanging out. The coach instructed the two
women to start playing a game of darts in order to attract attention.
The two women followed the directions to a tee, that is, they played
a game of darts. However, since they weren't actually interested in the
game, they kept to themselves, and their true feelings of boredom showed
through. Next, the coach took her turn. She pretended not to be very
good at playing, she exaggerated her interest in playing, she emanated
fun and invited the men in the area to assist in her—spurious—attempt
at learning how to play.

Now, this is game play, not the game of darts, but the game of
flirting. To be clear, I don't condone playing games with the emotions

of others. This, however, is the art of flirting which isn't to be done maliciously or taken overly seriously. It is meant to show an interest, without being false or deceptive.

Beauty

> *It's not what you look at that matters, it's what you see.*
> —Henry David Thoreau

Beauty is something we want: the woman, the car, the jacket. Ugly is something we don't want: the woman, the car, the jacket. But these things are subjective and not objective. How many times have you seen a dress on a woman and thought it was the most hideous piece of clothing you'd ever seen? But she thought it was beautiful, worth buying and wearing. Beauty and ugliness are individual characteristics and not social or universal.

We like to say, "Beauty is in the eye of the beholder," but we also say—usually about a mismatched couple—"Love is blind," the implication being you wouldn't date that person, so clearly she or he sees beauty in the other. "Ugly is in the eye of the beholder," too.

Many items are measured as beautiful or ugly. There is the obvious, physical appearance; however, the less obvious—emotional, intellectual, beliefs, values—all interact to create, to various degrees, items we know as beautiful or ugly. We can control or influence both

Continued on Page 69

Once the men joined the game—both games, of darts and flirting—the coach introduced her students. The students made small talk with their new found friends, and then one of the women confronted one of the men by saying, "Have you accepted Christ as your savior?"

Now, I firmly believe in, and advance, the idea people need to get to know each other, and themselves, in order to have an honest, meaningful, and healthy relationship. However, there is more than one correct way—and a great many more incorrect ways—to go about this. This woman's move was a bit premature in my opinion. "There is a time and place for everything," and though you need to be clear about what you are trying to achieve, you also need to decide when and where to ask the hard questions. There may not be a "best" time and place, but you need all three conditions: clarity, time and place, not just one or two.

Many people think if you're looking for marriage, you

should make that clear as soon as possible in the relationship. But remember, marriage is an objective, or goal, of a relationship. It's not the start of the relationship. When you look at a relationship from the point of view of the objective, you give the impression you are likely to accept, or even force fit, almost anything in order to reach your end. You may be more likely, or willing, to make concessions or sacrifices if your focus is overly biased by too few attributes. Remember the "end justifies the means"? This is a case of marriage being the "end" and the "means" being any available person, regardless of form or fit.

You need to be brave enough to ask yourself the difficult questions and courageous enough to answer those questions honestly, before you ask others to do the same. Most people don't like questions or being questioned because questions require answers, and answers require thinking, decision-making and commitment.

Continued from Page 68

beauty and ugliness, either directly or indirectly. We either alter the physical, emotional, intellectual, or belief, or we alter our perception of those characteristics.

In my experience, people have changed my perception of them. I have dated women who did not like certain aspects of themselves. Instead of changing what they didn't like or simply avoiding the topic altogether, they chose to focus all their, and my, attention on those issues. Over time, the problem areas were all I could see, because they were emphasized. Finally, I had to agree with their own negative assessments of themselves.

Beauty and ugliness are not static; they are dynamic, ever changing. Someone you thought to be beautiful yesterday may appear less appealing, even to the point of being ugly, today, because your perceptions have changed. Maybe you discovered the man you loved is a pedophile or murderer. Maybe the woman you loved beats her children. In other words, beauty and ugliness are personal preferences, and, as such, there is no clear definition for what beauty or ugliness actually is.

"Everything has beauty, but not everyone sees it," Confucius wisely said.

15

Asking the Questions

So if you are going to ask people questions to try to figure out their personalities, their motivations and actions, then you need to ask yourself these same questions. Three main components will help you get the best answers: thinking, decision-making, and making a commitment.

Thinking requires three steps: gathering, structuring and evaluating information. First, one must gather information, but not just any information, the pertinent information; then one must structure the information in an organized manner; and third, one must weigh or evaluate the significance of the information. In structuring and weighing the information, the individual may discover some information is missing or irrelevant. The difficult tasks are to determine which information is real or true, which information is relevant, which information is a distraction, and then to weigh the relative importance of each piece of information.

In fact, the task of gathering information often entails asking more questions, which means more thinking, more decision-making, and more commitment. It is a recursive process.

Decision-making requires three steps as well. The truth about any activity is the less often you do something the worse you are at doing it. Therefore, not making decisions often enough or not making the correct kind of decisions leads to poor decision-making skills and poor decisions in the future.

First, as with all things in life, you must begin slowly, with a reasonable magnitude. What I mean by this is to start with small decisions and work your way up. With familiarity, time, and reiteration, you progress to greater magnitudes of decision-making as well as learning how to make decisions more quickly. It is a learning experience just as it is with any other activity like baking a cake, riding a bike, or driving a car. Only with continued repetition do people have the ability to learn. If you are never repeating anything, then you are always doing everything for the very first time with no prior basis or knowledge.

Don't be discouraged. No one begins at the level of expert or even at the top of their own personal game. It would be highly unusual to achieve expert level the very first time you do something, anything. There is always more to learn and room for improvement. Decision-making requires picking and choosing from a host of options, thereby reducing the number of possibilities. The other options are not necessarily incorrect; they just aren't the ones necessary for the particular objective at hand.

The second step in becoming a better decision maker is to get feedback. In order to properly learn anything, accurate feedback is required. Most people do not get, or even ask for, feedback for their decisions. And the problem is when they do get feedback, they often trust or listen to others who are not qualified to give feedback, people who either really don't understand the subject matter or people who are no better at making decisions themselves. This is the proverbial "Blind leading the blind."

The third step in making better decisions is to go back and evaluate your decisions, giving yourself feedback. It's necessary to determine what you did correctly so you can do it again, and also to determine what you did incorrectly in order to improve or never make that error again. The process of this evaluation either by others or by yourself requires asking yet more questions and being open and vulnerable to criticism.

The truth is you cannot determine your future course of action if you do not honestly evaluate your past performance. That is my definition of learning.

You might have already realized making decisions means making commitments, committing to the information you gathered, and committing to the options you have chosen.

So why is commitment such a scary word for most people? People fear commitment because once a commitment has been made, they feel trapped. They feel they cannot change their minds or positions, as if changing would be lying to or betraying themselves.

The False Concept of "Best"

Some fear commitment because they believe there is a "best," that once they are committed, something better may come along and they will lose out on a different option. You recognize the person who cannot decide where to eat because everything sounds good or nothing sounds good. This person believes there is a best choice, and he will be frustrated by making less than the "best" choice.

But this is a false idea. "Best" could be restated as "perfection." We define perfection as a singular, clear, unequivocal, unquestionable choice; there is no other, not even equal, idea. However, most people will be quick to understand the concept of "perfection" is not practical and cannot be achieved in reality. If perfection doesn't exist, neither does "best." Bad advice comes from a society of fiction, fantasy, and marketing which uses the singular model of perfection.

Yet people are always using this false model of "best" or "perfect" or "favorite." What does it mean to be the best? For example, if someone asks your advice about which is the "best" automobile, how can you answer? It all depends. What use does the automobile have? For many people, an automobile is more than simply a means to get around. It's also a symbol of who they are. So we have differing objectives, and we need to use different criteria to measure whether or not an item can even be used for the desired purpose.

I don't have a "favorite" anything. I may have a preference, because a situation may "favor" one item or choice over another, but that is not the same as a "favorite," which would be some item or choice I would choose no matter what the situation.

Whether we're aware of it or not, fiction and, of course, fantasy use this false concept regularly. We adore super heroes like Iron Man and action heroes like James Bond, who are the "best" at what they do. But it's ludicrous to imagine one person mastering weapons, martial arts, languages, and mathematics and still find time to be an accomplished sky diver, yachtsman, or race car driver. Fiction and fantasy are an escape from reality, not a substitute for it or a guide to it.

Marketing uses the concept of "best" in order to sell products, goods, and services. Imagine one razor satisfying every need, in every situation. It cannot be done.

This concept begins to influence, then, our own relationships. As we go about our day and work through our friendships, business meetings, and so on, we do things our own way, and we, of course, believe we wouldn't do things less than the "best" way; therefore, our way must be the "best" way. This leads to believing everyone else is doing things in an inferior manner, causing friction between individuals as each tries to push his or her own idea of "best" onto the other person.

There are many ways to do things incorrectly; as you can imagine, there is always more than one way to do anything. How we accomplish a task has to do with the objectives, the resources, and the situations. The idea of correctness itself is subjective, not objective. Following is an example of a way in which my girlfriend and I almost caused a minor friction between us.

I was loading the dishwasher one afternoon when my girlfriend commented on the way I put the utensils in the basket. I placed the knives, forks and spoons with the heads down. She pointed out the possibility of the utensils aligning with each other, spooning as it was, and interfering with the cleaning process. I pointed out my rationale was safety because a person could get cut or skewered with the business end of the utensils jutting out. We had different perspectives, reasons, and rationale, none of which were incorrect. After considering her suggestion, and since I was the only person who would be unloading the dishwasher and facing the menace, I decided to load the spoons and forks up but the knives down.

From time to time this idea of "best" or "favorite" is used against you. A psychological attachment occurs when a person chooses a specific option or point of view. You have made a commitment and would therefore look like a liar, hypocrite or fool to be seen changing your selection. Once you have committed to a "best" or "favorite," the other person may try to hold you to that choice. By using the Dichotomy Model of extreme opposites—"right versus wrong," "true versus false," "good versus evil," "Madonna versus Whore"—they or you may discount or disregard all the other possible options. In other words, one implies, "If you are for this, then you are, also, automatically, against that," even if the two items are mutually exclusive. This psychology is so significant lawyers use these tricks to their advantage in courtrooms, salespeople use these tricks to influence your purchases, and worst of all, you do it to yourself.

I was talking with a woman one afternoon when she asked me what one thing I looked for in a woman, implicitly determining my "favorite" feature. I tried to explain people are much more than any single item, or physical attribute, but she persisted, almost trying to force me to give her whatever answer she was seeking. She seemed to get annoyed I wouldn't play her senseless game. I felt as if she were intentionally trying to back me into a corner in an attempt to justify her perception of men: "That's what all men must want." She seemed to be acting this way for one of three reasons: to gloat all men are shallow and she is above all men, or possibly to boost her own low self-esteem if she felt that she measured up, or to justify her own low self-esteem if she didn't.

The Dichotomy Model is extreme, overly simplistic, immature, and, therefore, false logic. In psychology, this type of logic is conceptualized by "splitting," a defense mechanism which works in and on relationships. An attitude of "all or nothing" leads to drastic and unstable oscillations. The inability to reconcile, or integrate, the reality that people and situations are not one dimensional but have multiple facets and therefore have elements of both positive and negative runs counter to the cohesion necessary for healthy relationships.

The next time someone tries to push you to choose a single item out of many equally desirable choices, or tries to simplify things to a dichotomy, be cautious of their motives, and be aware of the ramifications.

The Dating Industry

Life is slightly more complex than a simple "yes" or "no." There is no singular, all encompassing, absolute, correct answer or way of doing things. But we unconsciously transfer this concept of "best" to our selection of partners, either looking for or wanting to be the "best."

Unfortunately, the industry of providing relationships thrives on bad advice and misinformation because there is a conflict of interest between people looking for relationships and the business interests of dating sites. Think about it: dating is big money, but people pay only as long as they are *looking* for a relationship. Once people on the site find their relationships, they have no further need for the site and the site loses income. Therefore, dating sites don't have a clear motivation to find relationships quickly for their clients.

Dating sites also have conflicts within their own philosophy: they point out there are many people, and many matches, available on their sites, yet they conversely subscribe to the "one, and only one, true love" ideal. They prosper by promising clients they will find their "soul mates." Misinformation perpetuates sales and the need for even more advice and help. But if the existing advice were proper and useful, we would all have good relationships and there would be no need for any more advice.

Many relationships fail because of bad advice and conventional wisdom which people have been socialized to accept and believe. We keep doing the same things over and over, using the same bad advice and incorrect conventional wisdom, and then we wonder why we don't get a better outcome.

And herein lies the problem with the concept of a "Soul Mate," "the best person for me," and "the one and only." If there is always something or someone better, you end up searching perpetually. No matter what you do today, there will be something better tomorrow. So why do anything today? Simply wait until tomorrow when it will be better. Where is the end to this logic, where is the beginning, and when is it good enough? This search for perfection creates a stifling, even debilitating, effect of not being able to move forward, or not getting anything done for fear of not choosing "the best" possible option.

People often get to a point of "Analysis Paralysis" where there is simply too much information to process. They say, "Where do I start?" Ask any salesperson who can recount the many customers who simply could not make up their minds because they kept going back and forth between the different possibilities.

Studies have shown people who live in small towns or small communities are more able to find a partner than those living in large cities due to "too many options." Not being able to separate the relevant from the irrelevant, or the significant from the insignificant, as well as the expectation of the "best" or the fear of "not picking the best," which is treated as a failure, causes the inability to even begin the process, much less complete or excel at it.

Getting Past Fear

Getting past fear is crucial to thinking and making decisions. Fear is the lack of self-confidence, and self-confidence is greatly affected by the understanding, or lack of understanding, of failure. There is always the fear of choosing an (the) incorrect option(s) because we're afraid of failing. But society does not understand the true meanings of "failure" or "success." Unfortunately, this misperception of "failure" begins at an early age, with parents. It is one of the greatest problems with the school system.

Our perception of failure affects every person, every day, in almost every way. Why we think what we think, how we think what we think, and what we think are all affected by it. Why, how and what we do (or don't do) or achieve comes down to this perception of failure.

The truth is "failure" is natural: your first steps were a failure, your first words were a failure. Think of the many maxims great people have created to deal with the effects of failure:

- "We learn a great deal from our mistakes."
- "We learn more from our failures than from our successes."
- "Failure isn't an option, it's an imperative."
- "Don't be afraid to fail; we, all of us, do it often and regularly, and we are all the better for it."

The accepted definition of failure, of not succeeding as a singular act or event, is incorrect. There is a great difference between failing and not succeeding; they are not at all the same thing. You may lose a battle, but you haven't lost the war.

Failure is the act of quitting, giving up. As long as there is persistence, there is no end and, therefore, there can be no failure. In other words, if you haven't stopped, or until you stop, you cannot be judged as either a failure or a success. A society and school system which tells you not passing, or not succeeding, is the same as failing is doing you a disservice.

What I have tried to show in this section is asking and answering questions, that is, thinking, making decisions, and committing, provide the opportunity for both learning and teaching.

Poor, improper thinking, decision making, and commitment, with no or improper feedback, and no or incorrect learning lower self-confidence, and self-esteem, and lead to worse thinking, decisions, and commitments in the future. These ways of making decisions create stagnant conditions and even push us backwards.

Good, proper thinking, decision making, and commitment, with good, honest feedback, and learning raise self-confidence, and self-esteem, and lead to better thinking, decisions, and commitments in the future. Better thinking and decision-making actually propel us forward and make us better people.

———•◆•———

16
CHAPTER

Identity Roles

People's personalities are a combination of items: their genetics, their upbringing, meaning everything which is learned, and their situational influences. We like to posit "Nature versus Nurture," as if they are exclusive opposites, but both contribute to who we are. Nature refers to inherited, genetic, or chemical (such as hormonal) causes. Nurture refers to learned causes. Studies have shown nature and nurture contribute approximately fifty-fifty. We don't, and can't, imagine a human being without nature any more than we can imagine a person without nurture.

Nurturing means what we begin learning in childhood. Learning is facilitated by imitation, emulation, or expectations. The ways in which we are treated by the people around us directly affect the ways in which we see ourselves and will respond to various situations in the future. As our parents are the first and primary contacts in our young and impressionable lives, they have a significant initial impact. If your parents treat you poorly, you will see yourself in that light; alternatively, the opposite treatment may result in a person having overconfidence.

Nature and nurture actually matter a lot. However, it might not be the nurture of the parents, but of society which affects us more. Our social and economic situation, in great part, dictates what we are exposed to, and, therefore, affects the way in which we see the world around us. We cannot learn that which we are not exposed to in some way.

For example, in the late 1990s, the U.S. Department of Education studied Early Childhood Longitudinal Study data. In *Freakonomics*, the authors identify which factors help determine school success and which don't matter. The ones that mattered most came down to the IQ, education, and socioeconomic status of the parents. The ones which didn't determine school success were parental actions, such as taking a child to museums or reading to the child. While it's true children tend to resemble their parents to some extent on just about all personality traits, this finding doesn't demonstrate the nature versus nurture debate adequately because parents and children usually share both genes and environment.

For example, studies show twins often exhibit eerie similarities in personality and habits even when raised apart in different countries.

However, these anecdotes don't provide enough evidence to determine nature versus nurture. While genetics are very important to personality, shared environment exerts at least some influence on childhood personality though this influence fades once children leave the household and interact with teachers and peers.

For example, people will either imitate or emulate their authority figures if they agree with them, or rebel if they disagree with them. When you rebel, you're rejecting what your parents and other authorities say or what they stand for. You look for other people who are more like you in an attempt to validate yourself, your view, and your feelings. This is where peers come into the picture. Peer pressure itself is neither positive nor negative; it has to do with how it's applied. If your peers exhibit what are considered good qualities or attributes, then society accepts, even pushes you toward, those peer pressures.

Many people argue parents hold the entire responsibility for personality traits and behaviors of a child. Parents are only part of the issue. Peers have a significant influence over one another, even more so than parents. The influence of peers over parents is heightened because people relate and identify with people who look like, or who they believe are like, themselves.

For example, if you've ever seen two toddlers who see each other, even for the first time, it is obvious they are drawn to each other. Their similarity in appearance creates a connection: "Hey, you look like me, so you must be more like me than those big people."

As we develop into adults, our inherited traits and preferences exert an increasing influence on our environments both actively, as we select and create our own environments, and passively, as when people treat us differently. And, over time, our inherited traits exert a greater impact on the development of our intelligence.

The Nurture Assumption

Researchers have been unable to find any child-rearing practice that predicts a child's personality, achievements, or problems outside the home. Even when parents treat children the same way, they turn out differently. For example, there is no correlation between the personality traits of adopted children and their adoptive parents or other children in the home as there should be if "home environment" had a strong influence. What's more, how children are raised—in day care or at home, with one parent or two, with gay parents or straight ones, with a stay at home parent or working parent—has little or no influence over personality. What parents do with, and for, their children affects children mainly when they are with their parents.

The Cinderella Effect

A parent's behavior toward a child affects how the child acts around the parent, but not how he or she acts around others. Children learn early on that they can reconstruct themselves away from their parents. What our parents do to us is overshadowed by what our peers do.

For example, turkeys have some fixed patterns. If they hear a cheeping sound, they will bond with whatever is making the sound, thinking it is a baby. It is called a fixed action pattern. A study done with a polecat and a turkey show the turkey will "love" a polecat if it cheeps.

Although this may seem funny, and you are not a turkey, another study showed the simple use of the word "because" triggers a yes response. When people waiting in line to use a copier were asked if another customer could cut the line, they were turned down forty percent of the time if no reason was given. However, if the request used the word "because"—even if the reason was nothing more than "Excuse me, I have five pages, may I use the Xerox machine 'because' I have to make some copies"—ninety-three percent of people said yes. This is a fixed action pattern in humans or a conditioned response.

Interactions

People act in one of three ways in each of their interactions with others. These roles are dependent on what you have learned, imitated, emulated, and come to expect and how you learned those traits.

1. Authoritative / Dominant / Confident

Parents, mentors and other authority figures provide role models for the child. They define a pattern of how to act or react given certain situations of authority, superiority or leadership. This is a self-assured, confident, position.

2. Compliant / Submissive / Unsure

Parents, mentors and other authority figures teach children what is expected of them both individually and socially. People have personal, individual expectations as well as societal expectations. They learn how to act or react given certain situations of subordination, obedience or inferiority. If the expectation is "Do as I say, not as I do," a position of uncertainty is created.

3. Mature / Neutral / Independent

People are capable of independent thought, a melding

of various different preexisting ideas. Nothing is actually original or new; there are simply complex combinations of prior knowledge. In some cases, by combining old information, one comes up with new concepts which may contradict the imitations or expectations previously ingrained.

The point of defining these various types of interactions is to describe what happens depending on the role each person takes in a relationship, and, more specifically, to show that a particular situation may have very different outcomes.

For example, my buddy Eric called me one day after talking to a man he does business with. Eric complained the man had taken a stern tone and an authoritative position. While Eric recounted the conversation to me, I noticed a particular theme of authoritative/compliant. Knowing about the relationship Eric had endured with his father, I recognized Eric had, in that conversation, returned to his childhood. He felt he was being scolded all over again. Here was a grown man being made to feel like a child, expected to be compliant.

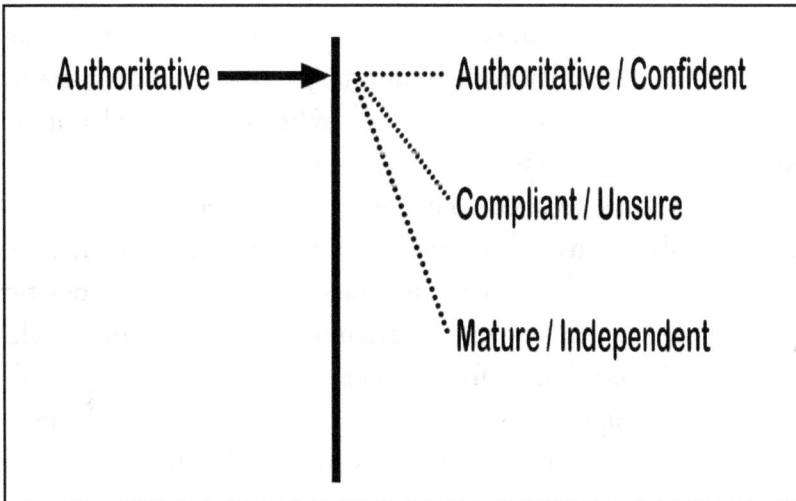

Because most of us never get to be seen by our parents as mature, independent, authoritative people in our own right, we don't learn how to respond properly when we are placed in a similar authoritative/compliant situation. And there are people in society who count on this automatic response to authority in order to take advantage of children and adults alike.

Now, there are certainly situations in which one person should act as the authority and the other person needs to be compliant; however, there are situations where this dynamic is entirely inappropriate and not acceptable.

A limited number of combinations can exist between two people, each of whom has a specific role. Imagine one person beginning a conversation from the place of authority. If that light were to pass through a prism it would split, falling on (or viewed by) the other person in one of three roles: authoritative, compliant, or independent.

From authoritative to authoritative creates a dynamic in which both people are intent on exerting their role as the authority figure. This leads to a butting of heads and a great deal of discord or, at the very least, a lack of harmony. From authoritative to compliant, and vice versa, creates the familiar dynamic of a parent-child or a leader-follower relationship, which may or may not be appropriate. From authoritative to independent creates the dynamic of condescension, which can easily deteriorate to ill will.

From compliant to compliant creates the dynamic of comrades. Depending on the particular situation, this may be acceptable; however, over time, typically, a leader will emerge. When no clear leader or guide flowers, bickering or resentment may follow.

Interactions between compliant and independent may create a dynamic similar to that of younger siblings attaching themselves to an older sibling, or a patient becoming attached to a caregiver. Sometimes this is appropriate; however, this dynamic can also be the result of neediness, which can lead to frustration and strife.

Relationships between mature independent and mature independent are treating one another as equals. This dynamic may take the form of a situation in which every person excels at an appropriate time rather than having a singular consistent leader and follower. Alternatively, it may result in a mutual, shared consensus.

To understand what kind of interaction you can expect, Coach Stephanie McKenzie suggests, "Have people tell you about their parents. Both the relationship between their parents, and their own relationship with their parents. What did they learn from those relationships, and therefore what are their expectations of new relationships? Don't accept or be fooled by the vague, evasive, or politically correct answers. Our past does not define us, but it is what sets us into motion."

Remember, your parents, as well as all of the people around you, are molded by, and products of, their environment. The various people in their lives have affected them in many of the same ways as you have been affected.

So the next time you are having a conversation with someone, notice whether they present themselves as the "Authority," a "Subordinate," or an "Equal" and be sure to notice how you, in turn, respond to them.

(This chapter was informed by Berne.)

17
CHAPTER

The Actors

Along with Identity Roles we take on, there are Actors who appear in our relationships. Generally, three actors show up in relationships, appearing in times of or creating stress or drama.

- The Victim
- The Antagonist
- The Savior

These three rely on each other; one cannot exist without one of the "partners" to complete the transaction. The Antagonist cannot exist without someone to Victimize, the Savior cannot exist without a Victim to save, and the Victim needs an Antagonist, a Savior, or both.

Any person is capable of being any actor or acting in ways different from what is "usual," depending on the specifics of the situation. Age or stature isn't a prerequisite, or determinant, for how we act. These are learned behaviors, which is to say they come from our past, typically our youth.

Victim

One of the actors we encounter in our lives is the Victim. A victim is an unwilling participant, a person harmed, physically or emotionally, due to the actions of others, or events outside of his or her control. This is a person burdened with cruel or unjust impositions or restraints of authority or power, subject to a burdensome or harsh exercise, a duty or misfortune that causes hardship, anxiety, or grief.

However, two subclasses of victims exist who are essentially self-defined victims. One is the Martyr, and the other is the Exploiter. Both of these are willing participants in their suffering and burdens.

A false victim is a self-proclaimed victim, someone who imagines, or claims, others are treating him or her unjustly and uses the status of victim for personal gain. Self-proclaimed victims deny responsibility; fault always lies with someone else, or they claim the situation is out of the self-proclaimed victim's control. Often, or typically, the infliction is exaggerated. This position may be a learned behavior from childhood, either a defense or manipulation mechanism.

For example, a parent who perceives himself as a victim may project his own lack of self- assertion or control on to his children. He teaches by example that any attempt to overcome an oppressive situation is futile. The way the parent acts may be a projection or transference of his own self-worth: "If I (the parent) am worthless, then you (the child) are worthless." Alternatively, the parent may victimize the child as a way to offset the victimization the parent feels from other sources: "Since my boss made me feel worthless, then I will make you feel worthless. Because I can't argue with my boss, I'll take my frustration out on you." A parent who is a victim may also fall victim to the child, as the child may perceive the parent as weak.

Antagonist

Every victim needs an Antagonist, real or perceived, a person who subjects others to hostility or ill treatment, actively opposing or acting hostile to someone or something. The antagonist harasses or annoys persistently. The victim is persecuted. She is an adversary.

However, the antagonist may not necessarily be oppressive; the antagonist may simply inhibit the victim from pursuing a course of detrimental action. The persecution may be exaggerated or embellished and non-existent. The victim may be putting on an act in order to attract attention.

By the same token, an antagonist needs a victim. Antagonists need to exert control over someone else in order to feel in control of themselves. Some antagonists may be looking for the gratitude of the victim, someone helped by the structure the antagonist provides. In some cases, the antagonist may inhibit the victim's negative impulses, or actions, and may actually help the victim in the relationship. In these cases, being an antagonist, or aggressor, is not necessarily negative.

For example, parents who stop their child from running into the street or their teenager from doing drugs can be seen as oppressors, aggressors, or antagonists from the child's perspective. The child may take the role of a self-defined victim when, in reality, the parent is acting on the child's behalf and for the child's benefit.

Savior

The Savior saves others from an imminent danger or a potentially distressing situation. These types of people either cannot or do not differentiate between actual victims or self-imposed victims. The savior keeps the victim from being lost or abandoned.

A savior always needs a victim. The savior requires someone to save and thereby feels needed or validated. The savior sees herself as the opposite of the antagonist.

However, not all victims need a savior; not all victims want to be saved. They don't actually want their situation to be altered. In some cases, the victim is seeking only the pity, sympathy, or ability to manipulate and play on the emotions of the savior. And some saviors are looking for the undying gratitude of the saved victim. In some cases, the savior may become an enabler or actually sabotage the victim in order to continue the savior—victim relationship.

For example, as the savior, or rescuer, a parent who does not give a child the opportunity to face his own dilemmas may instill in the child the belief that by claiming to be, or acting as, a victim, the child will get whatever he wants, that he will get his own way. I'm not saying children should be left to fend for themselves. That would be the opposite extreme, one of being inattentive, because the parent must provide guidance in, and lessons on, how to resolve issues.

Saviors may take the form of the person who brings home stray animals. In women, we may see the person who wants to save the alcoholic man, or the woman who wants to change the bad boy. This is often called the Florence Nightingale effect.

In men, we may see the person who wants to save the alcoholic woman, or the man who wants to save the stripper or prostitute. These men want to be the Knight in Shining Armor. (Think of the movie *Pretty Woman* in which Richard Gere, a billionaire, goes after Julia Roberts, a prostitute. Does that not strike of a Savior!) These people want to save others from their own destructive ways and may actually seek out those with problems, or in need, even if the problems are self-inflicted.

But a savior can become an enabler, too, in order to keep the victim trapped in the status quo. After all, once a victim is saved, there is no need for the savior. You don't continue to go to the doctor once your illness is cured. In fact, the savior is likely to be abandoned once the victim recovers.

For example, alcoholics and drug addicts are told to remove themselves from both the situations and the people who entrapped them, contributed to, have influence over, or remind them of their addictions. That ultimately includes saviors, as the duty of a savior is after all, temporary. Once an alcoholic stops drinking, his or her status as victim-in-need changes; he is no longer, directly, consistently, in stress. At that point, the savior doesn't have anyone to save; she has served her purpose. The savior is likely to feel useless in the relationship. The now ex-victim isn't in need and will begin to feel resentful of the savior's continued attempts to give direction, or the ex-victim will resent the savior's over-compensation abilities she employed because of the perceived inabilities of the victim.

Once a person with low self-esteem or low self-worth is boosted to the level of adequate self-confidence, he or she will be strong enough to find more or other potential partners. In other words, dating someone with low self-esteem with the idea that you will help the individual come out of a shell and, therefore, he or she will be forever indebted to you, may backfire. The individual will likely question why staying with you makes sense. After all, you are interested in a person with low self-esteem, which makes the two of you incompatible, even at odds, with each other. This may not be your brightest move.

Leaders

Antagonists and saviors are closely related because they are strong-willed leaders. An antagonist has the ability to be a savior, also, and vice versa. A person can antagonize those who are not in their group and save or protect those who are, or would like to be, in their group. A person who initially takes the role of antagonist can later become the savior. For example, if the victim complies and accepts the antagonist's instructions or does as the antagonist wants, then the antagonist is also the savior. By the same token, the initial savior can later become the antagonist if the victim doesn't follow the savior's instructions or do as the savior wants. In some cases, the Savior and Antagonist are played by the same person: the Savior who is an Enabler will often decry the very actions they themselves are enabling. This makes for the ultimate Victim: "I'm just trying to help!" or are you?

How Gender Affects Actors

Gender may play a part in how people are patterned to behave, and how they are expected to respond, as well as how their actions are interpreted. More conventional wisdom and bad, unrealistic, unreasonable, advice creates false expectations and incorrect interpretations of actions.

Men are trained from a young age to be aggressors while women are trained to be saviors. Men are expected to be dominant and hunt: go after the female, who is expected to be submissive, to the point of being the victim of the males' attack.

Think of the conventional wisdom you've heard about gender interaction:

- "Don't take NO for an answer!"
- "Women don't really mean what they say or say what they mean."

At the same time, men get the opposite message, which is women are soft delicate creatures to be cared for, saved.

- "Treat her like a Princess."
- "Boys are snakes and snails and puppy dog tails."
- "Girls are sugar and spice and everything nice."

This dichotomy may lead to the woman, the victim, being fought over by one Aggressor and one Savior, to be won like a prize, with no say of her own.

So should men attack women or save them? Both of these extremes amount to dysfunctional expectations and actions. Men should do neither and neither should women take on the role(s) of either victim or savior.

Instead, avoid acting, or getting involved with actors. Assess the situation and behave accordingly.

Aggression is the last action of the weak or hopeless, and many Victims act victimized "By Choice not Chance." You cannot save someone from himself.

Actors need a play. And Drama makes the world go 'round.

———•◆•———

(This chapter was informed by Karpman.)

18
CHAPTER

Drama

E very narrative involves the actors discussed above and conflict, which moves the story forward. Without conflict, there would be no change. The conflict is played out as drama between actors. Some amount of conflict or drama is a good thing, but, as with everything, too much of one thing is good for nothing.

Our lives are full of conflicts and dramas of varying degrees, but drama creates upheaval, which makes it imperative for you to spot, identify and deal with dramas, especially the ones you yourself create.

Fairy Tales

Fairy tales are an excellent source of conflict and drama. For example, in "The Pied Piper," the hero begins as the rescuer of the city and the persecutor of the rats, then becomes the victim to the mayor (a persecutor), and in his revenge becomes the persecutor of the village children. The mayor is the victim of the rats, then the rescuer in hiring the pied piper, then persecutor of the piper, then the victim when the children die.

In "Little Red Riding Hood," the heroine begins as the rescuer by bringing food and supplying company to the grandmother. Then Red

Riding Hood becomes the victim to the Wolf (a persecutor), who falls victim to the woodsman (a persecutor), who, as savior, rescues Little Red Riding Hood and the grandmother.

Cinderella is doubly persecuted by the stepmother and the stepsisters, then triple rescued by the mice, the fairy godmother, and the prince. She is then persecuted again, after midnight, and rescued again by the prince.

Combinations

As you can see, the same person can act in many different ways, depending on a combination of Identity Role, Position, or posture, and Dramatic Role.

For example, extra-marital affairs can be described in terms of an antagonist, a victim, and a savior. The person seeking an affair may be characterized as a victim, real or perceived, in search of a savior. A person may see, or paint, their partner as an antagonist, possibly using justifications such as she or he doesn't understand me, care for me, love me, pay enough attention to me, fulfill my needs, or abuses me either physically or emotionally, and so on. These justifications may or may not be factual. They may be the imagination or exaggerations of a self-defined, self-proclaimed victim. The external partner is the savior coming to the aid of, and rescuing, the victim.

For men, it may be the damsel in distress to their Knight in Shining Armor.

For women, it may be the misunderstood bad boy, who simply needs the love of a good woman to change his mischievous ways.

Overprotective parents, or parents who are in denial of their own child's shortcomings, may act as savior to the child. The parent may accept all the responsibility for the child's actions, in effect accepting the punishment the child may rightly deserve, or they may blame others for their own child's actions. In either case, the child is not made to deal with the ramifications of his or her own behavior. This in turn may foster the continued behavior in the child to act as an exploiter, manipulator, and victim.

Some women are victims of their husbands: abused, physically or emotionally, by aggressors. At the same time, the women may be saviors/protectors of the children, getting between them and their fathers.

What do we make of the child who is abused and victimized at home only to become the aggressor, bully, to others? The victim of one person may be the antagonist of another person. The reversal of roles may be an attempt to gain some perceived control over one's own life.

The person who is abusive or antagonizing to coworkers, wait staff, customer service representatives, cuts you off in traffic, and so on may be acting out due to being the recipient of abuse, or perceived victimization, from others, and he has feelings of no control over his own life. These behaviors are one way of gaining perceived control.

Of course, some people thrive on drama, so they create stressful situations. In some cases, it creates attention, making them the focal point. They may feel any attention is better than no attention.

You cannot control positive attention; you can't always get other people to recognize you, and even if they do, it may not be in the way you want. On the other hand, you can control, at least to a degree, negative attention. You keep pushing until you get a response: "I'll keep going until you do something about it." Even children realize it's easier to get negative attention than positive attention.

When the body is under stress, hormones such as adrenaline are released. We get excited, our heart rate increases, and our breathing becomes rapid. So drama gives us a shot of legal drugs. At some point, people may crave these excursions of excitement in their lives.

So it's worthwhile to realize the next time you are watching your favorite television show, or arguing with someone for no apparent reason, both of which seem to incite some sort of anxiety in you, you are a drug addict in search of your next fix.

Yes, you can be a couch potato and an adrenaline junkie all at the same time.

Are you addicted to dysfunction?

All drama is based on the values we carry in our baggage. So let's examine what values are and how you define yourself through your values.

———•◆•———

19
CHAPTER

The Value of Values

If you don't know what is important to you, how will you know if the people in your relationships—business and social—are right for you?

If you don't know what you believe in, then how will anyone else know? If they don't or can't know, then how will the two of you relate to each other?

Values have many other names you may be familiar with; ideals, beliefs, morals, ethics, and so on. Our values define us at our core, but most people never take the time to explore what they believe or why they might believe it. People's ideals, beliefs or values are greatly influenced, molded, and shaped in their childhoods by their socioeconomic circumstances and by their parents. The social status, the education level and the financial health of the parents within, and relative to, the community has, in some cases, a direct or indirect and a positive or negative, effect on the children.

We tend to take for granted, and thus become complacent about, those things we have easy access to, and we place a high value on those things which are scarce or which we have difficulty attaining. For example, those who don't have access to financial security place a mythical power on it, whereas people who have easy access to finances wonder why others simply can't seem to get their hands on money. As the great playwright George Bernard Shaw said, "The man with a toothache thinks everyone happy whose teeth are sound. The poverty-stricken man makes the same mistake about the rich man."

In other words, if you don't have *my* problems, then you must not have *any* problems. I place a high value on those things in my life I find significant; at the same time, I devalue those things in your life I find insignificant.

The theory behind "Values" consists of the understanding there is a set of core beliefs, recognized in cultures across the world, which can be classified and categorized. Taken individually, each ideal may seem reasonable; however, in the grand scheme of things, no one person agrees with, or even accepts, all of these core ideals. Some of the ideals even conflict with one other because people may have opposite views of them. This should come as no surprise.

Our ideals are our priorities in life, those things in which we are willing to invest our time and possibly for which we might even make sacrifices. So we must weigh each ideal against all of the other ideals in order to clearly determine which ones are of the utmost importance or significance to us. And to decide which ones are not.

What Type of Values Do You Have?

Are you understanding, appreciative, tolerant, and protective of the welfare of people and of nature in general? Do you believe people should have equal opportunities in life? If this describes you, then you have Universalism tendencies.

Do you feel loyal to friends? Do you devote time to the people close to you? Do you care about the well-being of those around you? If so, then you have Benevolence tendencies.

Do you easily share your interests and activities with the people close to you? Do you take pleasure in the company of others? If you answered yes, then you have Intimacy tendencies.

Do you accept the customs, processes and procedures of your society and of those people close to you? Do you have strong religious affiliations? If so, then you have Traditional tendencies.

Do you restrain your actions, inclinations and impulses which are likely to upset others and violate social expectations or norms? Is it important to you to "follow the rules" even when no one is looking? Then you're described as having Conformity tendencies.

Do you actively avoid those things in your environment that might endanger your safety? Do you place harmony and stability of society above personal freedoms? If so, then you have Security tendencies.

Do you want to be respected and to have others follow your directions? Do you want social status and prestige? If you answered yes to these questions, then you have Power tendencies.

Is it important for you to be "recognized" for your accomplish-ments? Is it important to you that your occupation, education and income demonstrate your success and competence according to social standards? If so, then you have Achievement tendencies.

Do you like to spoil yourself? Are you self-indulgent? Do you have fun and seek pleasure for the sake of gratification? Then you have Hedonism tendencies.

Are you unconventional, non-conforming, sometimes rebellious? Are you adventurous, a thrill seeker? If so, then you have Stimulation tendencies.

Do you pride yourself on your creativity and your independent thought process? Is it important to you to do things your own way? You probably have Self-Direction tendencies.

Types of Values

Universalism: understanding, appreciative, tolerant.

Benevolence: loyalty, devotion, caring.

Intimacy: sharing, pleasure in other people's company.

Traditional: accepting of society's customs, strong religious affiliations.

Conformity: restraint, following the rules.

Security: mindful of safety, stability of society above personal freedoms.

Power: desire for respect, leadership, social status, and prestige.

Achievement: desire for recognition of accomplishments, success in society.

Hedonism: self-indulgent, seek pleasure.

Stimulation: unconventional, sometimes rebellious, adventurous.

Self-Direction: creativity, independent thought, doing things your own way.

What is the point of these questions? We need to understand our values are so important to us as individuals that they represent *limits* and *boundaries* we don't want crossed.

Once we determine our individual values, we can examine our motivations to decide how we're communicating with those around us.

And here's where one of the myths of relationships comes into play.

———————

(This chapter was informed by Schwartz.)

20
CHAPTER

Myth — What's Age Got to Do With It?

Modern society has many obsessions: looks, wealth, fame, status, power, weight, and the list goes on and on. Youth, or the lack thereof, is somewhere on the list. How does age affect love?

When we are young, we want to look, act and be treated older than we really are. Later on in life, we want the entirely opposite treatment. From the age of approximately four to approximately eighteen, individuals are grouped and categorized based strictly by a number, their age. The separation of people by age begins early on in life and is ingrained into individuals all throughout school. This segregation creates false assumptions and expectations because it uses an incorrect metric as a differentiator between individuals.

This false differentiation causes a lifelong effect on people. In fact, once out of school and in the work place, this entire dynamic is challenged. We find that people of various ages may be leaders as well as followers, for example. At some point in a person's life, her direct manager will be younger than she is, or you may have to answer to a customer younger than you are. This situation may cause distress or conflict internally or externally because it doesn't follow the tradition so clearly driven into our belief system: age is what defines us, differentiates us and what matters.

How important is age?

A friend had met a new girl, funny, sweet, good-looking, and from all accounts, the first few dates went well. They liked each other and had similar interests. They laughed and seemed happy together. Suddenly, my friend had a change of heart. He decided he didn't like her as well as he'd thought and broke off the relationship. When I asked him why, he said he discovered she was older than he. He was adamant age wasn't the issue, but it was at that point he began to notice their incompatibilities.

I enjoy travel, so does that mean everyone my same age has traveled? Do all people my age enjoy the same music, movies, and books? Exactly how much must we have in common in order to be compatible? If we carry it too far of course, we can only connect with ourselves.

What exactly does age represent?

We have five ages, chronological, physical, emotional, intellectual, and zeal.

Chronological is obvious; it is ticks on the clock. Physical is our health and well-being. I work out regularly, so according to *Men's Health* magazine, my physical health is mid-twenties. If you don't work out, eat unhealthy foods, smoke and drink, your physical health may be older than your chronological health. Emotional age is our sentiment, our attitudes and our filters. You may have heard of an "old soul." This is someone who seems to be wiser, more compassionate and sympathetic than his or her chronological age would suggest.

Intellectual age is our knowledge and the ability to reason. We have the saying "She is wise beyond her years," suggesting someone who seems to understand situations beyond what is usual considering her chronological age. Zeal is our outlook on life. We sometimes say about a person that "He's young at heart." Zeal for life doesn't depend on chronological age. You can have it at eighteen or eighty. Or you may not have it at all.

Each dimension of our age is independent from the others. In each facet, we learn and grow differently; we advance at differing rates because our own unique experiences dictate how, and how quickly, we age. Although there may be some correlation between our chronological age and the other age facets, the connection is not nearly as strong or clear as we imagine.

Of the five ages, we have control over four. The only one we have no control over is chronological. It's ironic that the one age we can do nothing about is the very one we use as a measure of who we are.

If you met a person you were able to connect with on two, three or four levels, physical, emotional, intellectual, or beliefs, but he or she was outside of your age range, would you reject the connection? Would it make sense for you to do so?

Chronological age is only as important as the parties to the relationship make it. The more you live in your past, the more important chronological age will be. Living in the present reduces the significance and the effects of age. For example, it isn't uncommon for some women, for various reasons, to prefer the company of men a few years senior. How much of an age gap is acceptable is entirely personal and not a universal issue. A person who chooses someone considerably outside of the typical societal age range is simply more extremist, rather than actually deviant.

In a time when people in general are more health conscious and are, therefore, more youthful, it shouldn't come as a surprise that the "acceptable" ranges of age are widening for both men and women.

Similarity of values and depth of knowledge are what are important to relationships, regardless of the chronological number, that is, assigned by scientists. We have some control or influence over our physical, emotional, intellectual and zeal age. As the saying goes, "Don't judge a book by its cover." Just because the first publishing was some time ago does not automatically make the material inside unimportant or insignificant. So, too, it goes for individuals. If we enjoy many of the same things, believe in many of the same ideals, hold many of the same values, what more could you ask for? A specific number of which neither of you can do anything about? A little known secret is many people don't see themselves as their age, the number; they are "who" they are first and foremost.

Albert Einstein once said, "Not everything that counts can be counted and not everything that can be counted, counts."

———•◆•———

21
CHAPTER

Motivation

Motivation has two drivers, desire and fear. We are always moving toward something or away from something. The confusing aspect for human relationships is that from the outside, the result of an action often does not convey the underlying motivation. As I pointed out earlier, these opposites—in this case, desire and fear—actually manifest themselves in identical ways.

For example, some people want a relationship because they desire some aspect of the relationship. However, there are those people who seek out a relationship as a result of fear of some other situation. They choose a relationship as "the better of two evils."

Some people see their jobs as an extension of themselves, their careers, but others view their jobs as simply a way not to starve. Similarly, those who want an intimate partner may appreciate the attributes of the other person. But some view an intimate relationship as an avoidance of being alone.

A recent study of couples shows a high number of people stay in relationships they're unhappy with in order to avoid what they see as the worse alternative, being alone. But those of us looking at relationships from the outside—without knowing the underlying motivation—will come to incorrect, even opposite, conclusions about why two people are together. We may say, "They must be in love." When we don't know or understand the underlying cause or motivations of a person's actions, we are more likely to be prejudiced, make assumptions, or come to incorrect conclusions.

The problem is many people actually don't know their own motivations, desires or fears.

You believe you know yourself, the way you are; you believe you know your likes and dislikes. This is called the "introspection illusion." Experiments show introspection is a fabrication. We look at something we did or how we felt and then create an explanation for that action or feeling which we believe to be rational.

Researcher Tim Wilson did a series of experiments in which people had to choose between items or rank them. However, when participants were asked to explain their choices and they had to think about and justify those choices, many changed their choices. (Here is another example of first choices, once examined, that needed to be changed. In other words, people make quick, impulsive, inaccurate decisions they wouldn't have made had they simply taken the time to think through them.)

Of course, people also lie about their motives, even with the veil of anonymity. Some of the reasons people lie are fairly obvious: the motivation of gain, desire, loss, fear. Less obvious reasons are there is no motivation to tell the truth, no gain (no desire) or there is no reason not to, no loss (no fear). People often lie to others simply because they are lying to themselves. This may be done to protect self-esteem or to avoid conflict, internal or external.

If we agree motivation is driven by either desire for or fear of something, then we must have a clear understanding of our own desires and fears. Only then can we understand our motivations for actions and feelings.

We may think we can control our desires and fears, but influences all around us create false desires and false fears. For example, advertising and marketing use these principles extremely effectively to herd the population to companies' desired niches.

Understanding Motivation

In order to understand our motivations, we need to understand how we are influenced. Automatic response mechanisms are either natural reflexes or learned responses to given stimuli, situations or questions. Many of these "automatic" responses are directly linked to a person's upbringing, learning based on the social situation in which a person was raised. Some of these responses are imitations of authority figures; others are social expectations of the compliant identity (as spelled out in the identity development chapter). Additionally, social proof, or peer pressure, is the reasoning behind "might makes right" where "might" does not necessarily mean physical power, but the "might" of numbers or quantity. For example, when someone follows the crowd or the leader, or complies with "Just do as you are told and don't ask any questions," or one is persuaded "All the girls do it so you should, too," she is obeying "might makes right."

Influences on our motivations abound. It is necessary to break down the phalanx of influences so you can recognize them and counteract if you need to. Only then can we figure out our own desires and fears and thus our motivations.

We like to imitate Authority: the people we recognize as authorities create expectations. Experts, authority figures and people whom we respect have a great deal of influence on us. We expect people who have devoted their lives to one specific topic to know more than we do, so if we agree with the authority figures, we are good or right and have found our motivation. For example, in meeting with the doctor, we may take the position "He or she is Right" and, if I agree, then "I am also Right." This is an ego boost because now you are as smart as the expert. On the other hand, if I don't agree, then "Maybe I'm Wrong," but if I listen and learn I can transition to "I am now Right." Now you joined, and became a member of, the expert group.

However, sometimes our expectations carry over to areas in which the knowledgeable person is not actually an expert nor is he or she any more knowledgeable than we may be. For example, simply because a person has a Ph.D. in economics, which is mathematics, doesn't qualify him or her as an expert on social matters. So perhaps this expert shouldn't influence my motivation for a certain activity, like voting for or against a particular social program.

Scarcity motivates us: if it is rare it must be special, so if I have it, I, too, will be special. Many people want status, to be recognized, or to be set apart from the crowd. Possessing those things which are rare makes us rare. Therefore, working harder to obtain those items others don't have is proof we are worthy.

Reciprocation, societal sharing, and obligation motivate us. If we never received anything in return for our efforts, then we would feel our efforts were worthless. We wouldn't be able to gauge whether what we were doing was worthwhile, meaningless, or even harmful. This is not to say what we get in return must be equal or even returned by the receiver. When we donate to charity, we don't need material items in return. We may accept as a validation of our compassion, the gift of gratitude or self-satisfaction. Some of us are motivated by the idea that "A rising tide lifts all boats," what benefits society as a whole is likely to benefit the individual as well. In any case, we need to know what we are doing actually makes a difference, and this is done by some form of reciprocation. It is a feedback mechanism that motivates us.

Some people are motivated by Self-Commitment: reinforcing to ourselves and others that we are who we say we are, and that we can be counted on. For example, when I rollerblade, which is often, I use traffic hand signals even when there is no traffic or other people to see them. I signal "Turning left," "Turning right," although I know no one else will be affected. I do it not for others but for myself. Making those traffic hand signals is a commitment to me: I am telling myself, "You are turning; you can do this." When I do that which I promised I would— turn—I build my self-confidence. I follow through with what I set out to do; I was successful. The tree may fall in a silent forest with no one to hear it, but at least it knows it fell.

In general, people don't give themselves enough credit for their accomplishments. But the reason for this is not modesty; they don't literally commit to it in the first place. You can't hold yourself accountable for your own success if you don't consciously perpetrate it. Committing to an action or a feeling creates its own motivation. Remember, decision-making is committing.

Even a thing as seemingly inconsequential as Consistency can create motivation.

Consistency is how you learned how to ride a bike, drive a car, operate the television. Our world would be chaos if it weren't for consistency; nothing would or could get done. More importantly, consistency is the basis for trust, how I know you will do what you commit to. When deeds match words, an expectation arises that predictable results will follow. Being consistent can be its own motivation, simply to do what you say you will.

Taking on Challenges motivates some people. We are always growing physically, emotionally, and intellectually, whether or not it's obvious or drastic. Challenges bring on this growth, like drama but with much less stress. If we stop challenging ourselves, and thereby stop growing, we become stagnant, complacent, uncaring, and even hopeless.

Money as a Motivator

Money itself is not a motivator; it is a vehicle used to achieve an end. If it were a motivator, we would all be sleeping on mattresses stuffed with dollar bills. Material ends, such as objects, power, achievement, and security, can all be attained or measured by money, but they are only things to move us toward what we desire or away from what we fear. Power represents control, lack of power is then lack of control; achievement represents respect earned, lack of achievement is then lack of respect; financial security, either literal or figurative, is peace of mind, lack of financial security is then lack of peace of mind. Do you, or does someone you know, seek money and power in order to gain control or is it for the purpose of not losing control?

You'll notice some of the influences I've listed correlate with the causes of, or persistence of, bad advice or incorrect conventional wisdom.

Automatic response: a mechanism which allows bad advice and incorrect conventional wisdom to be accepted so easily, without any thought at all. "Just Do It."

Authority: the so-called experts must know best, and if they don't, then who does?

Social proof or peer pressure: if enough people say it's so, it must be.

Scarcity: implying only those few, special, deserving people are worthy of getting it, such as sacred or holy knowledge. Therefore, you are a part of, and accepted by, the in-the-know crowd.

Reciprocation: you get as much, or as good, as you give. Therefore, the more you give, or the better you give, the more you expect to receive in return.

Consistency: when the advice or conventional wisdom aligns with the way we want to see ourselves and others, we are comforted to think we know, even if it is incorrect.

Challenge: the more difficult to attain, or obtain, the more it must be worth.

The bottom line is by understanding and manipulating these base motivators, others can get you to do things not in your own best interest. Therefore, it is best you understand the motivators in order both to spot manipulators as well as to determine why you do what you do and direct yourself.

What are your motivators?

————•◆•————

(This chapter was informed by Cialdini.)

22

"You Need to Communicate"

Once we figure out what our motivations are, we can communicate on another level. However, even though almost every person giving relationship advice states, "You need to communicate," this isn't advice at all, not any better than the obvious "buy low and sell high."

The question, then, is what *is* communication? Is talking non-stop for hours about the weather communicating? Is telling someone about all your problems communicating? How can you communicate to others that which you don't know or haven't thought about yourself? If you aren't sure of your feelings, your needs, your desires, how can you convey them to others? And what should you do when one person makes an effort while the other person avoids, evades, or actively tries to thwart the effort? I know from experience asking questions of those who don't want to deal with or face an issue gets you nowhere; instead it may lead to deception, conflict, or actual miscommunication.

Furthermore, is all communication good or valuable communication? Is communication restricted to one form of interaction or interplay only?

If it were so easy to "communicate," why wouldn't everyone already be doing it?

Clearly, you'll need to be prepared before you can even make an attempt to communicate.

Forms of Communication

It's useful to know, for example, there are three different types of communication: visual, vocal and verbal.

Neuroscientists assert approximately fifty percent of the human brain is for optics, sight, and its interpretation. It should come as no surprise then that approximately fifty-five percent of communication is visual, thirty-eight percent is vocal, or tonal and inflection, and the remaining seven percent is verbal, the words you actually use.

What this means is first we see, then we hear, and only then can we interpret.

Don't misunderstand: even though verbal is only seven percent, the words we choose are extremely important because they tell how we relate to each other, how we see ourselves, how we see the other person, and how we see us as an entity. If I use "I" too much, then I'm narcissistic; if I use "you" too often, then I have low self-esteem; if my speech doesn't include "we," then we aren't a team, we aren't in this together.

In fact, a study has shown a correlation between people who use "I" more than general speech demands and heart disease. People who focus on themselves exhibit narcissistic tendencies. Narcissistic people place a high degree of stress on themselves, in part by trying to keep up the appearance of how they see themselves. Stress leads to heart disease; therefore, the over use of "I" is a predictor of heart attacks.

The verbal is very significant. It just happens to make up a smaller percentage than the rest of how we communicate.

But we don't really need statistics to explain the weight of the communication types. We can easily observe clues such as visual cues go a long way. Even animals communicate visually and vocally!

Here's an example: I was in the park, yes, rollerblading, and I stopped to talk to a bicyclist. A car drove by, and a dog in the car barked at us. Bob, the bicyclist, made a face and said he felt annoyed when a dog barked at him. "Wait," I said. Then I explained I knew the owner, Bobby, and the dog, Audrey, a black border collie mix with white markings. Audrey only barked at me when she was in the car, never when she was outside on the leash and walking with Bobby. Visually, Audrey's tail was wagging, a sign of contentment, not contempt. Her ears were relaxed, not pinned back, and she was not baring her teeth, both signs of aggression. As for vocally, her bark was light, not low and throaty or growling and menacing. In fact, I thought I understood the communication to be, "They are out playing; why can't I get out of this car and play, too?"

If we paid more attention to how people, and animals, say things, we would get a great deal more out of our conversations. Ask a dog if it wants to go outside and see the response. How does it know what you are saying? Are dogs that much smarter than humans that they can learn our language? To a degree. Your "language" is in your actions and in your tone. They simply pay more attention to us than we do to each other or for that matter to ourselves.

Wouldn't it be nice if humans gave us the visual clues dogs do? When someone became upset, his ears would go back, clearly telling the conversationalist, "I am not listening to anything you have to say." And yet they do. People give visual clues all the time.

I was at lunch with my friend Eric one day at a restaurant when I noticed a couple, a woman and a man, sitting at a large table. She was leaning across the table talking. Her eyes were wide and her mouth was tense. She gripped a napkin in one hand and motioned with the other. The man leaned as far back as he could while still sitting at the table and not falling over in the chair. His hands were in his lap and his face looked closed: his eyes never met hers, and he didn't smile or talk.

I said to Eric, "Watch this; there is something very wrong happening here."

Soon, the tears formed in her eyes and then rolled down her face. He moved further away. Surely, he was breaking up with her.

The visual—body language and their facial expressions—had said it all.

And yet we don't even pay attention to ourselves. Of course, we can't see our own facial expressions, and we rarely reflect on our posturing, and we don't notice our tone of voice. In effect, we miss most of our own clues, so it is a wonder we can communicate with each other at all.

One of the main reasons emails, texts, and Twitter create problems is because we're only getting the seven percent of communication. There is no visual or vocal to give us a context for the verbal. Don't get me wrong. I'm not against the use of emails, texts, or social media; however, technology is a tool just like any other and when used improperly, these tools can be dangerous. These devices have their time and place. They aren't meant to be used for all communication every time and in every place. In fact, the over-use or misuse of these communication techniques hinders good communication. Since good communication is one of the keys to a good relationship, it behooves you to be good at it.

Styles of Communication

Communication contains two major aspects which combine to create four possible exchanges: clear or unclear (masked), and direct or indirect. In addition, there are two manners in which words are used: a general, broad, sweeping, conceptual manner or a narrow, specific, detailed, tangible manner.

An example of communication which is *unclear and indirect* is the following: "Someone should do something about this situation." "Someone"? Who exactly? Do "something"? What exactly? The action, either required or expected, is unclear. If the individual is referring to cleaning up the room, what is the action he desires? Should I throw everything out, burn it, shove it in the closet and under the bed? Give me a hint.

Unclear and indirect speech allows the speaker to escape accountability. It also allows the listener to shed responsibility: "If I don't act on this, I cannot be held accountable because you may be directing this at someone else."

Unclear and direct includes the words "you," "I," or "s/he" "should do something about this." At least I know who needs to do something although I still don't know what needs to be done.

An example of *clear and indirect* is "Someone should take out the trash." I know what needs to be done, just not who you think needs to do it.

The only proper *clear and direct* communication would be "You should take out the trash." I know who needs to do what. There is no hidden message or agenda. Clear means leaving no doubt; obvious or unambiguous; having or feeling no doubt or confusion; leaving nothing to chance; and no chance of misinterpretation. Direct means going straight to the point; frank; bearing immediately and unambiguously upon the facts at issue; labeling unambiguously those people or parties involved.

Clear and direct is the healthiest form of communication. Since the best style of communication is clear and direct, three out of the four possible styles are obviously inadequate.

In terms of clear communication, we notice people generally state things in terms of either what they want or what they don't want; rarely do they state both what they want as well as what they don't want. In terms of direct communication, many people think being direct is rude, but you can still speak with civility or tact without being rude. The correct way to be direct is choosing your words wisely.

As the saying goes, "Say what you mean, and mean what you say."

If you don't speak clearly and directly to me, don't get upset and be surprised when I don't respond in the way you expected. A person refers to a couple who is having martial issues and then asks me what I think about it in order to find out if I want to marry her. But my responses will be in the context of their failed marriage, not what I think of marriage in general, or marriage to her in particular.

Have you asked or been asked encoded or encrypted questions in an attempt to get some information slyly, unknown and undiscovered? And how often does this backfire? Either the deception is discovered or the answer is to the actual question, which isn't what you expected.

How many times have you listened to other people talking, watched them become more and more upset with each other, and thought, "They aren't even talking about the same thing."

Even when we use the very same words, the manner in which we employ our words has a significant impact on how those words are interpreted and understood.

For example, when we use words in a general manner, we are being figurative, whereas when we use words in a narrow manner, we are being literal. In this way, the same words will convey different meanings. The person using a word literally will likely have a specific scenario in mind. This literal use limits the application of the word. The word "marriage," for example, will have a different meaning to the person who is using it in a broad social context as opposed to the person who is thinking of a specific marriage.

Communication Behaviors

How we *behave* during our communications is strongly linked to the visual and vocal. Your behavior influences the ways in which others interpret you and your motives.

For example, if you lean in, then you are listening, and the other person knows it. If you're talking to someone and the two of you start breathing similarly, you're connecting, mirroring each other's actions. Conversely, if one of you is talking slowly and the other is speaking quickly, then your breathing patterns cannot be the same. When speakers adapt their nonverbal behaviors to match those of their speaking partners, they indicate they are accommodating and of like mind. The "chameleon effect"—the unconscious mimicry of the postures, facial expressions, behaviors, and mannerisms of one's interaction partners—draws speakers together. The chameleon effect applies to language as well: matching acoustic features such as accent, speech rate and pitch suggests you're "on the same page." One hypothesis is matching acoustic features in conversation aims to gain social approval from others. Linguistic mimicking is also linked with trust; even in an online chat room environment people will mimic certain words, phrases, and punctuation.

Physical behavior affects the way in which you do and don't communicate with others. In some cases people may be quiet participants, and in other cases, they may be vocal participants. Common terms used to describe these two extremes are "passive" or "aggressive." Making this judgment or assumption without understanding the underlying facts and motives may lead one to incorrect conclusions, both about the individual and about the communication taking place. In truth, one may not be passive but simply diffident, that is listening intently, which is still active in the exchange. Also, one may not be aggressive but simply assertive, that is passionate with regards to the topic. The combination of the two extremes may lead to the familiar "passive-aggressive" type of behavior, a "push and pull" rather than a "give and take."

Allow me to explain these four terms.

Passive means not reacting visibly to something that might be expected to produce an emotion or feeling; not participating readily or actively; inactive.

Aggressive is defined as vigorously energetic, especially in the use of initiative and forcefulness and is characterized by or tending to unprovoked offensives, attacks, invasions, or the like; militantly forward or menacing, an active participant.

Assertive suggests being confident in one's own ability; worthy; self-assured.

Diffident is quite different from passive: lacking confidence in one's own ability, worth or fitness; timid; shy; restrained or reserved in manner or conduct.

As communication is expressed in a combination of the three, visual, vocal, and verbal, people may be passive or aggressive in any one or more of their expressions. The difference between being passive and diffident, or aggressive and assertive, is their respective motives. Whereas the "passive-aggressive" style of communication is negative and dysfunctional, the "diffident-assertive" is not.

Just because someone gets excited doesn't necessarily mean they are being aggressive, just as someone who is being quiet may not be passive, but paying attention. All too often, people assume the extreme or apply those labels in an attempt to discredit the speaker.

Similar to these behaviors, we may come across others as being extroverted or introverted. The fact is people are not fully one or the other, but rather their situation will affect their style of communication a great deal.

If you are highly confident about or competent concerning a subject, you may express yourself openly, but confronted with a topic you know nothing or little about, you may behave reservedly, cautiously.

Sometimes extroversion may be expressed as either aggression or assertion. People who are confident may be labeled as being aggressive when, in fact, they are being passionate and simply assertive. You will recognize aggressive people as those who push their point of view or agenda on to other people. Assertive people inform other people of their point of view.

Introversion may be expressed as either passivity or diffidence. People who are reserved may be seen as being passive, that is not participating or not taking an interest, when they are actually diffident. Passive people do not take part in or contribute to a conversation, whereas diffident people actively pay attention and are involved.

Of course, passivity and aggression can be affected by the situation; even a cornered cat, having nowhere to run, will lash out.

Behavior into Words

It turns out similarity attracts when it comes to communication. In a study of 187 heterosexual speed dating participants, researchers found language similarity directly correlated with romantic interest and potential relationship stability. The study looked for similarities in a face-to-face conversation and instant messenger chat. Participants were scored on a "Language Style Match" scale. Of those with a score above the median, over thirty-three percent were mutually interested in contacting one another; of those who scored under the median, just over nine percent wanted contact. Speed daters were three times more likely to match with their date for every standard deviation increase in the Language Style Match. (In statistics, the standard deviation is a measure used to quantify the average, typical, amount of variation around the mean, the average, or the expected value, of a set of data. The average is a single number; however, in practice, there is always some variation, deviation, around that number. In this case, for each standard deviation, the average variation increase above the mean, the stronger the match.)

The study of the Instant Messenger (IM) chats of eighty-six couples who had been, on average, dating 1.31 years was followed up three months later to predict relationship stability. This study sampled ten days of IM chats and assigned a Language Style Match score. For every standard deviation increase in Language Style Match, couples were approximately two times as likely to be together at the three-month mark. Those who scored above the mean were found to be over seventy-six percent more likely to be together at the follow up.

These studies suggest you are more likely to become involved and stay involved with someone whose use of language is similar to your own. It isn't just behavior then, but the actual words you choose which makes communication valuable.

By being aware of how we present ourselves and how the other person responds to us, we can increase our ability to communicate effectively. Take that John Gray, "Men are from Mars, Women are from Venus."

External Factors Affect Your Perception

Studies show people who are forewarned of potentially ill-tasting food automatically find that food to be, you guessed it, bad. The same food is judged good even when the questionable ingredient is divulged after the tasting.

Women who are reminded of the stereotype "Females are not very good at math" tend to score worse on math tests. However, Asian women, who are reminded of the stereotype "Asians perform well on math," perform better.

Warm sensations are projected onto a person. For example, if, upon meeting another person for the first time, that person is holding a warm coffee, individuals found that person to be nice, generous, and caring. If the person were holding an iced coffee, he or she was perceived as difficult, stand-offish, and hard to talk to.

Your expectations influence not only how you perceive others but yourself as well; you prejudge. People translate their physical world into words, then believe those words.

———◆———

23
CHAPTER

Communication Interplay

Now that we have seen the different types and styles of communication, we can begin to understand communication as an "interplay," a series of actions and words depending on knowing ourselves and one another. Each communication interplay is a combination of people's personal perspectives, their identity roles, their actors, their values, their motivations, and their communication styles and behaviors.

But communication as a whole follows an order. First, we must *understand*. Understanding requires listening. We can't understand that which we haven't clearly and properly heard.

Only after understanding can we *accept*. This isn't to say understanding means we *will* accept what is said. However, how can we accept that which we don't understand?

Once we accept we can *agree*. We can't agree with that which we can't accept.

> ## Communication Depends On
>
> **Form:** Visual, Vocal, Verbal
> **Style:** Clear, Masked, Direct, Indirect
> **Behavior:** Passive, Diffident, Aggressive, Assertive
> **Interplay:** Understand, Accept, Agree

For example, you may say the earth is flat. I can understand both the meaning and the rational; after all, Texas is rather flat. I can accept how one may have this point of view. If one hasn't traveled or if this information doesn't have any importance, significance, or relevance, it seems reasonable. However, I can't agree with this position as I have information and knowledge to the contrary.

A major problem in communication is people don't follow this sequence when talking with others. Because the order is ignored, bad advice and incorrect conventional wisdom gain footing. People accept ideas which they themselves don't understand or they accept meanings without asking questions. Once accepted, they can begin to agree with those things they really don't understand.

The following fable explores "miscommunication" based on incorrect interplay.

The Blind Men and the Elephant

It was six men of Indostan,
To learning much inclined,
Who went to see the Elephant
(Though all of them were blind),
That each by observation
Might satisfy his mind.

The First approach'd the Elephant,
And happening to fall
Against his broad and sturdy side,
At once began to bawl:
"God bless me! but the Elephant
Is very like a wall!"

The Second, feeling of the tusk,
Cried, —"Ho! what have we here
So very round and smooth and sharp?
To me 'tis mighty clear,
This wonder of an Elephant
Is very like a spear!"

The Third approach'd the animal,
And happening to take
The squirming trunk within his hands,
Thus boldly up and spake:
"I see," —quoth he— "the Elephant
Is very like a snake!"

—John Godfrey Saxe

There are two perspectives (or six in the case of the blind men): that of mine or my group, and that of yours or your group. A person's perspective is his or her personal point of view. That point of view is crafted by, and colored by, one's social and economic past as well as by the many people in that past.

In the first attempt at interaction, one wants his perspective to be heard and understood.

Typically, initially, we begin with a calm sense both our perspectives will be compatible if not correct. However, this isn't always the actual outcome. When disagreements, misunderstandings, or rejection occur, stress and distress are elevated. We assume we are not being understood and, therefore, we must intensify our efforts. This intensity can be interpreted in different ways by the other party and, depending on the identity role and communication style one assumes, may be seen as adversarial, aggressive. The harder we try to be understood, the more frustrated we become and, therefore, the more intense we become.

It may be the other person understands. However, perhaps he or she does not accept your point of view. One of the clichés of our time, "Which part of 'no' don't you understand?" shows up our own misunderstanding. Pets, children, telemarketers, co-workers, all understand what no means; they simply don't accept your no.

So we need to ask ourselves and the other person if a situation of misunderstanding occurred or if it is one of non-acceptance. Continuing to "persuade" or argue an issue as though it is misunderstanding when it is actually non-acceptance can have no other effect than to escalate the intensity and concomitant frustration and eventually lead to anger.

Those people who want complete and total agreement expect and require a surrendering of what they see as their opponents' views. They are domineering, they don't listen, and they have little or no regard for the other person's past experiences. They feel their point of view is the only correct or meaningful one. These over-bearing people appear to have an attitude of winning at any cost.

But, of course, the attitude of "me" or "my way" is a singular point of view and is not conducive to a "we" or "our way" relationship. In other words, this attitude is actually anti-relationship because it isn't likely any two people who come from different backgrounds would, or should, see everything eye to eye. When we focus on only one perspective, our own, and forget there are many others which need to be considered—and are equally valid—we paint the world in one single color.

When we see things from one, and only one, vantage point, the picture is extremely limited. Studies have shown we literally fille in the blanks with what we believe shoude be there. We see words that aren't, or automatically correct words incorrectly speled, we assume events or actions that never occurred. (Did you notice the misspelled words, the word omitted?)

Then, we tend to believe what we perceive. Our view point has a great deal to do with not only what we actually see but what we *think* we saw. And depending on what we think we saw, we use this imagined information in order to make decisions, and decisions are our judgments.

Often, our perspective gives way to our judgment, which is why and how we see things the way we do. People make judgments very often and very quickly. In some cases, this is best to avoid danger. A loud noise may cause one to jump or react impulsively. Judgments being expectations based on prior knowledge have to do with our perspective, experience and knowledge.

This prejudgment or rush to judge stems from certain physical and/or emotional triggers.

Prejudgments may be a defense against a threat or impending danger. The physical senses are mainly how we avoid danger. Sight: we see danger approaching at great distances. Sound: we hear disturbing noises at lesser distances. Smell: we can smell noxious odors within a few feet. Touch: we feel alarming sensations at arm's length. Taste: finally upon us, we can savor putrid, spoiled substances.

However, in low-risk situations, this overly-simplified method of assessing a situation or a person can lead to extreme characterizations which, once explored in detail, may prove to be completely incorrect. People judge each other based on visual, auditory, and possibly olfactory clues prior to having any other information or without knowing anything else. In other words, all interactions, especially with people we have never met before, employ some degree of prejudgment, unconscious expectation or prejudice. We say something like this: "From past experience, real, or perceived, or related by trusted others, I expect people who look or sound or smell like this will act in some predefined manner."

Accepting an alternative view point is not typically achieved through modification of existing information. What we do is integrate or add new knowledge rather than alter our present knowledge. We rationalize, saying to ourselves what we thought we knew wasn't actually wrong; we simply lacked information. We can then create a larger, more inclusive model of the situation taking into account this new information.

It is necessary to note here the old knowledge is not expunged or forgotten; rather, it is assigned a lower weight or ranking of importance while the new information is given a greater weight. The new knowledge is more relevant and relates to or is more closely connected with other preexisting knowledge. The old knowledge may still be valid and useful in specific situations.

We resist change, in part, due to the fact it would mean some preexisting information and possibly decisions of the past were probably flawed and possibly completely incorrect. We may have difficulty resolving our existing information, what we think we know, with the new information. Some of our knowledge may be conflicting, incompatible or mutually exclusive due to the way we organize our knowledge. This is because people tend to separate and compartmentalize ideas or concepts; in this way, we cannot detect, much less correct, our inconsistencies.

Because of this compartmentalization and resistance to change, we cannot and do not change another person's mind. They themselves chose whether and how to modify their preexisting knowledge. In fact, it is best if any new knowledge is presented from the stand point of preexisting knowledge. If it is related to something the person already knew or believed to be true, it will more easily be integrated.

Outside forces don't change us. They do, however, lead or guide us once we ourselves decide to accept the guidance. For example, no one changes or cures a drug or alcohol addict. The addict must first choose to change or be cured; then, and only then, can others assist.

A person has to reach a point where their existing knowledge or way of life is no longer tolerable, not just unacceptable or uncomfortable. Just as different people have differing thresholds of pain, they also have differing levels of tolerance.

Unfortunately, many of us operate under what is called a "Confirmation Bias." We see the world through a filter which confirms our beliefs rather than challenges them. People like Glenn Beck, Rachel Maddow, Ann Coulter, and Keith Olbermann provide fuel for beliefs. They filter the world to match existing worldviews, and if their filter is like your filter, you like them.

During the 2008 U.S. presidential election, researchers analyzed purchasing trends on Amazon. People who already supported Barack Obama bought books painting him in a positive light. People who already disliked Obama bought books portraying him negatively. These people weren't buying books for information; they bought them for confirmation. We want to be right about our perspective, so we seek out information that confirms and validates our beliefs, and we avoid contradictory evidence and opinions.

In relationships, this means we must accept all relationships will have disagreements, some of which will never be resolved. However, relationships of all types cannot survive a lack of understanding, either due to not listening or not comprehending. This is because people need to feel they have been able to express themselves and been taken seriously, and others have listened, regardless of whether there is agreement.

As I have argued, the problem is many people do not or cannot communicate their needs or their wants. Many people don't know what they need or want; others have difficulty expressing themselves due to their individual communication styles and behaviors. Some fear confrontation because they have a more compliant identity while some create confrontation because they have a more authoritative identity. Others avoid communication all together as their perception of their situation, imagination, or fantasy is better than the reality.

You get to understanding by knowing your motivations, your actors, your communication styles and behaviors.

Acceptance, well that is icing on the cake, and agreement is the cherry on top.

———————————

24
CHAPTER

Myth — Men and Women are Different

We employ stereotypes because they are useful. They provide us with mental shortcuts so we don't have to recognize and analyze all aspects of every person, event and situation. We can quickly classify the enormous amounts of data surrounding us. But sometimes such mental shortcuts don't work for us. (Shortcuts are called "judgmental heuristics.") For example, the adage "You get what you pay for" helps us often, but not all the time. There is a story of a woman who couldn't sell the jewelry in her store. Finally, she got so frustrated she told her employee to sell everything at half price and just get rid of it. The employee confused the message and instead of selling everything at half, priced everything double. The stock was gone before the owner returned from vacation. The lower price gave people the impression the jewelry was cheap, but the higher price indicated greater value.

The problem is we use stereotypes for men and women, too. Throughout history segregation has been used to justify the mistreatment of the opposing group. The extreme examples are easy to remember: Hitler dehumanized and made a scapegoat of a single group of people—a stereotype—so everyone else felt it was acceptable to continue to treat them the way Hitler was treating them. During the Cold War, people talked about Russians as if they were from another planet. Some people talk about immigrants the same way today. Republicans and Democrats even talk about each other as if they weren't human beings. It is so much easier to treat your partner poorly when you don't see him or her as having the same end desires as you. Saying someone does something because "He's a man" or "What do you expect of a woman" is a cop out. Those dismissals make it easier to divest yourself of the relationship.

One prevalent stereotype is women are emotional and men aren't. Men are treated like they have no feelings and women are treated like they are emotional wrecks. Many television shows focus on humorous communication differences between husbands and wives based on this stereotype. The men in these shows talk about sports, eating, hunting, and gambling, the women about feelings, friendships, relationships, and home life. These shows typically depict men as less emotionally perceptive or "denser" than women. Indeed, surveys demonstrate even college students perceive men and women as differing in communication styles. They view women as considerably more talkative and more able to pick up on nonverbal cues.

Gender Equality?

Women are catching up to men in all areas. For example, female heart attacks are on the rise due to similar workplace stress.

When society tends to think only women have emotions about relationships, men's emotions get slighted. Studies demonstrate human behavior is not based on gender. For example, men and women show affection in similar ways and are just as likely as one another to be affectionate.

Another stereotype is that women are bad drivers, but statistically this is not the case. In fact, after controlling for the fact men drive more often than women, men still get in seventy percent more accidents than women.

There have been many mixed messages between men and women throughout history. In medieval times, there were many rants about women being insatiably lustful: the message was female desire needed to be controlled. Images from history like the succubus and witches added to this message. But on the flip side, the Victorian / Puritan view of women was that they were chaste saints. During that time, we believed women to be less driven by their libido.

So on the one hand, supposedly, women exhibit an evil sexual desire and on the other hand women demonstrate—or even allow—very limited, if any, sexual desire. This is where we get the proverbial "Madonna versus whore" complex so confusing to both men and women.

A great deal of bad advice comes from the so-called Gender War/Battle of the Sexes. When we call it a "war" or a "battle," we approach one another as adversaries. But we need to see each person as simply a human being. If you look at another gender and think they're nothing like you, then the relationship will fail.

Another problem with gender stereotypes is when we try to break them down, people become confused. For example, we're told women want emotional connection with men; however, if a man shows what a woman considers too much emotion, then the woman will be unsettled. But in a relationship free of gender stereotypes, women don't get to pick and choose when, how deeply, and in what manner men feel or how it is exhibited.

People are using the wrong metric. We use "gender" to explain our differences when it's more complex than that. The fact is gender doesn't determine a person's values, communication styles, or motives. Our social and economic past experiences and upbringing determine these things. We are also guilty of making up science to support our social customs and beliefs. For example, parental investment theory says that a woman is less likely to be promiscuous because she wants a steady mate who will be available to protect her "investment" (pregnancy, breastfeeding, birthing, and so on) in the child. A consistent mate is more likely to help her and her child survive and hence her genes will be more likely to be passed on. A man, on the other hand, or so our theory spouts, wants to spread his seed in as many women as possible because he'll have more offspring that way and more chance of his genes surviving.

This theory paints the age-old Madonna picture of the loving nurturing mother as if once a woman gives birth, she somehow loses her sexual appetites and desires as well as any other vices she may have. So no more smoking, drinking, drugging, carousing...oh, but wait, it is the act of sex that led to the condition in the first place. The truth is that nothing at all changes, and we all know it. How many unwed mothers of multiple children, women who abandon their children to be raised by relatives, or mothers who neglect and abuse their children, do we need to produce to rebuke this virginal, wholesome, halo wearing picture? How many studies will it take to prove that people don't instantly or easily change?

As for the men of the myth, apparently they run around screwing every woman in sight! This is nothing more than an attempt to explain away "Why Men Cheat." If that were the case, then since one man can impregnate multiple women at a time, and there are as many men as women, if every man simply impregnated just one woman, all the women in the world would be pregnant.

In fact, men and women cheat at approximately the same rate. (More on that later.)

So women aren't always the stay-at-home protectors. Some studies demonstrate females are not the passive ones. Female monkeys, for example, exhibit lust and aggression in sexual interactions and in fights. They will choose roaming males and discard them when they are bored. Sometimes, they have sexual liaisons with more than one mate in a single encounter.

The prevailing rhetoric is men enjoy porn, the debasing, dirty side of life, whereas women, being the chaste, innocent and pure flowers, can't possibly like such a thing. This is more of the Victorian, Puritanical, Madonna complex. However, regarding human females, Dr. Chivers' study on porn shows women's sexual desire is as "dirty" as men's. Men and women continue to be set apart in their behavior, not by science or actual empirical observation, but by the false image of the two being polar opposites.

Another stereotype is men can be abusive, but men are not the only ones to get physically violent and abusive. Statistics show women can be abusive to men as well as other women. Studies have shown female physical aggression on the rise: aggression between teenage girls is rising because they see it in movies, musical videos, women's sports, mixed martial arts, and so on. Furthermore, no one challenges physical abuse so it becomes more acceptable. One young woman I knew told me her girlfriend hit her in the head with a frying pan so hard she had to get stitches. Had the aggressor been a male rather than a female, he would likely and rightfully have been incarcerated. Regardless of gender, domestic violence in a civilized society should not be accepted.

Men are not more likely to express their anger physically. Men and women physically abuse each other at about equal rates although women are more likely to suffer injuries as a result.

The truth is both sexes are manipulative and aggressive. This has to do with an inability for people either to express their emotions—a lack of communication—or their feeling of not being listened to, taken for granted, not being understood, and their feelings, and, therefore, they themselves, not being valued.

Biased studies produce ingrained myths in society. Scientists and neuroscientists can find differences they're looking for. To go at a study saying let's determine how women's and men's brains are different is not scientific: it is an answer in search of a question, rather than a question in search of an answer.

Should Women Use Tools?

Vacuums, circular saws, food processors, socket sets, barbeque grills, and so on are all designed and engineered devices; they are all tools. The word "utensil" originally represented any household item of utility; indeed, the word utensil comes from the word "utility." The synonym for utensil is tool. The sense that men use tools and women use utensils is an example of how society has perverted words to be more specific than their actual meaning, giving the words themselves a quasi-gender connotation. As all of these items are tools, and they are all designed and engineered, there is no reason or rationale one can point to as to why one gender might choose one over the other. A woman with a circular saw is no more or less natural than a man with a food processor. Any task may be natural, rational, reasonable or "normal" if we examine the qualities of the task itself. The benefits participants perceive from carrying out that task have nothing to do with gender and everything to do with the individual.

When people speak about how men and women's brains are different, what are they trying to get to? The researchers overlook or ignore the brain's functionality and place too much emphasis on the structural details, but these details end up being insignificant. There are small differences: Females and homosexuals perform worse than men on tests involving three-dimensional shapes. But this makes no sense. The authors of the study neglect the fact that male homosexuals are after all, men. This uses the stereotype that gay men are really women in disguise and, by implication, that lesbians are men in disguise. But if that were true, then half of the gay women should be performing as well as "men." In other words, the fact that homosexuals are made up of both males and females means they should, on average, perform just like any other group. Clearly, what the researchers found has nothing to do with gender. If it did, then homosexuals, being and representing both genders, would have to follow the same pattern as heterosexuals.

Besides, when was the last time you said to someone, "I'm really attracted to you because you are good with three-dimensional shapes?" Is this type of difference relevant or meaningful?

Discovering Psychology discusses the small brain differences between the genders, and summarizes these differences are not significant. They have no real meaning. We tend to focus on the technical small differences instead of stepping back and looking at the big picture. If the two genders are so different, then why would you, should you, want anything to do with them? At the simplest of levels, the basis of this "theory" is opposites attract. You'd be better off dating, and connecting, with people of your own gender.

These so-called theories have real economic and political significance. If gender brain differences were factual, then that would justify things such as differences in pay between men and women, advancement of men versus women, child care issues and so on.

Of course, differences do exist between some men and some women, depending on the attribute. Likewise, differences exist between men and men as well as between women and women. The question is whether the differences are *relevant* and whether the differences are significant to the situation at hand.

Unfortunately, gender bias may play a significant part in one's treatment of or attitude toward others, especially an impressionable child. For example, a mother voicing a low opinion of men in general will have negative effects on her son, as he is a member of the group she is disparaging. A mother speaking badly of men affects her daughter, too, who will take those stereotypes as facts. Of course, fathers' opinions can affect sons and daughters as well. Thus the stereotypes are perpetrated.

The point is focusing on differences between men and women rather than similarities won't help you at all in finding a relationship. If you demonize the other gender, but want to be with a person, you've set up a situation where you can never succeed. People don't realize they're demonizing the other group, but then they make snide jokes and say things they've been taught are true about the other gender: "Women do such and such;" "Men always do this or that." If you're going "to date the people you hate, or to hate the people you date, your fate is hate."

Think about the rhymes you learned in childhood: "Girls are sugar and spice and everything nice; boys are snakes and snails and puppy dog tails." Girls play princess, and boys play soldier. This mentality bleeds over into our adult lives and ruins relationships. Each of us must treat individuals like they have feelings similar to yours.

If a woman understands a man wants a relationship/companionship, too, then things can be different between a man and a woman. The way you *get* there might be different, but you're trying to get to the same place. Once we understand differences, we can understand differences are not the result. They are the manner in which you aim at the result.

What are men and women trying to get to? We have different tools in our tool belts, but they're just tools to get to where we need to go.

For example, recently, an intelligent, savvy woman told me her husband, equally intelligent and worthy, vacuums and she takes out the garbage, chores which are contrary to what society considers "traditional" roles. Their situation may be frowned upon, or at least questioned, because society classifies these tasks as gender specific. This is yet another example of the gender war at work. These gender specific tasks are based on the prior generations' beliefs that men work outside the home and women work inside the home. Of course, today that simply isn't the case; but, in fact, gender specific tasks have always been done by one or the other member of a relationship. On farms, in previous generations, men and women did various tasks because it took everyone to make the farm workable. Or consider single people, widows and widowers, for example, who have to do all kinds of chores in order to survive. When men are, or were, away fighting wars or working, who ran the businesses, took care of the household and family and kept society stable? Women, of course.

In addition, this sense that tasks needed to be separate was based on the ownership of the property. As men owned the property, that is the home, women took care of it as the cost of living in it. But today property is co- or jointly owned, so both parties have a vested interest in the maintenance and care of it.

Consider the chores themselves: vacuuming is repetitious and constant. Activities with these qualities can be soothing if the participant chooses to view the activity as such. As the activity occupies the physical and not the mental, it actually frees the operator to think or not. Once the vacuuming is done, it is complete; there isn't anything else, and just as importantly anyone else, to contend with. In addition, this task allows for structure and organization, control over one's environment. Exercise is a similar activity. It has all the same qualities, yet society doesn't place a gender label on it.

Taking out the garbage requires a series of events and people and therefore requires a different mindset: a person must take the trash from the house, a different person must come to collect the garbage and then someone must replace the emptied bins.

So this woman's husband appreciates a) repetition b) mental freedom c) finality of the task and d) control over his environment regardless of what the task is. She, on the other hand, doesn't hold these attributes in the same high regard.

Aren't we all, each and every one of us, different from every other person? The list of individual attributes is so long that even identical twins aren't identical. Is every attribute of importance? Of course not; some are and some aren't. Different attributes may be of significance in one situation and not in another, causing inconsistent, even contrary, interpretations of what is considered the same and what is different.

Consider the myth that men and women don't speak the same language. This is insulting to both genders. A woman who studies architecture uses the same words as her male counterpart, just as a shoe salesman knows the correct names for women's shoes. However, many books on this topic, like Deborah Tannen's *You Just Don't Understand* and Gray's *Men are from Mars, Women are from Venus* exploit this myth to make men and women feel more different rather than more alike. In 1992,

Gray wrote, "Not only do men and women communicate differently, but they think, feel, perceive, react, respond, love, need, and appreciate differently. They almost seem to be from different planets, speaking different languages." His books have sold over forty million copies in forty-three languages and Gray has opened over twenty-five Mars and Venus counseling centers with the goal of improving communication between men and women.

Gray conducted no research to support his claims.

Luckily, other researchers have found evidence contradicting his assertions.

- A very small difference exists in the number of words men and women speak every day;
- A very small difference exists between men and women talking about matters of personal concern;
- A very small difference exists between who interrupts more often;
- Women are not more perceptive to nonverbal cues;
- Women are no better at accurately guessing the feelings of others than men are.

Another myth is women speak a lot and men don't, but a linguistic study of college students, which followed both men and women, discovered few differences. The students were given voice recorders, and their daily conversations were reviewed. There was no significant difference between the word counts. Differences have more to do with the topic of conversation, and the participants' interest in the subject as well as their willingness to contribute to the conversation mattered, than gender. No significant difference existed between the words used; a person's education and literacy was of significance, not gender.

Given males and females of like education, literacy, interest, and willingness, they will likely carry on a balanced conversation. Otherwise, we simply wouldn't be talking to each other. What would be the point? And nothing would ever get done.

Researchers have concluded the following in reference to the studies on differences in men's and women's language: "In evaluating these results, it is important to consider that, despite the comparatively large number of studies that went into the review, some of the findings are based on only a couple of studies with sometimes rather small language samples and only one text source."

And consider this: "Recently, Mulac et al (2001) summarized the findings of more than 30 empirical studies and reported relatively unambiguous gender effects for 16 language features."

You can prove this for yourself. Watch competition shows like "Survivor" or "Big Brother," and you'll notice in the beginning the men and the women always try to create a gender alliance. By the end of the show, those alliances fail as people realize they don't have as much in common with each other based only on gender. Most people would rather be with someone who is like them emotionally, intellectually, and or morally, instead of simply biologically.

(Aspects of this chapter were informed by Weintraub.)

Myth — Opposites Attract

The notion that opposites attract is a standard film, novel, and sitcom plot. (The technical term for attraction of opposites is complementarity.) If someone is so different from you, then why would you, should you, want anything to do with them, which is the basis that opposites attract, at the simplest of levels. But here is another myth exposed: opposites do not attract; values attract.

A personal example: my mother was Catholic and my father, Jewish. From the outside, people would jump to the conclusion they were opposites, and so opposites attract. This ignores what was actually important to the two of them: the fact each practiced his/her religion, even moderately, would indicate they both had a belief in God. And that fact was necessary for them in their relationship. If they had been true opposites, one would have been an atheist.

I imagine James Carville and Mary Matalin fit this mold. They are a well-known married couple invested in politics. Carville is a Democratic strategist and Matalin is a Republican strategist. On the face of it, you might think this is a case of opposites attract, but this is a misunderstanding of the underlying attraction. They have a shared belief in working within the governmental system. It appears each would rather be with a person with opposite detailed views of what to do within that system, rather than be with someone with the same views and a disregard, or disrespect, for the system itself.

However, the myth of opposites is very strong. Studies have found seventy-seven percent of undergraduates agreed that opposites attract in relationships. Building on this myth, many dating sites configure their matches in such a manner. Harville Hendrix, Ph.D., of "Soulmatch," states, "It's been my experience that only opposites attract because that's the nature of reality."

However, research evidence suggests, well, the opposite (pun intended). Dozens of studies demonstrate people with similar personality traits are more likely to be attracted to each other than people with dissimilar personality traits. Similarity is also a good predictor of marital stability and happiness, especially of the personality trait known as "conscientiousness."

The "like attracts like" conclusion extends beyond personality to our attitudes and values. One study shows the more similar someone's attitudes are to ours, the more we tend to like that person. Biologists Buston and Emlen asked 978 participants to rank themselves on ten characteristics they look for in a long-term mate. They then asked these participants to rank themselves on the same characteristics. The two sets of rankings were significantly associated.

Again, so much for a Ph.D.'s expert opinion. His is a case of not understanding the underlying mechanism at work. People may look opposite on the surface, but they themselves may not truly understand their attraction because they aren't trained in analysis, after all. Therefore, self-reporting, such as that done on match-making sites, is futile.

You have to admit you don't know what's opposite. If you don't know what's important to someone, you don't know what's opposite for him or her. What is truly important to you is what is attractive in the other person. You are the equal and not opposite.

You've heard the saying "Birds of a feather flock together." This one happens to be closer to the truth of relationships than most. For example, when is the last time you thought to yourself, "I want to join that group of people; they're nothing at all like me" or "I'm pro-choice, so my best partner will be anti-choice." Really?

Opposites do not attract, values attract.

———•◆•———

26
CHAPTER

Myth — Play Hard to Get

Playing "hard to get" is one of the myths many people receive when they ask for love advice. But, like many of the pieces of advice I've examined in this book, it's a bad one. For example, research suggests men are less interested in women who are "standoffish" than women who are receptive to their advances. Of course. Which would you choose: the job that wants you or the one that doesn't? If there is a hesitation or trepidation on the part of the employer, that should signal a caution, warning, signs of what is to come. It's probably just a matter of time before the employer finds something wrong with you or someone else he/she is better in touch with. I take the view that if you don't want me, I don't want to force myself on you.

I saw a commercial for coffee which showed a woman on a train, drinking said coffee, looking happy, relaxed, almost in heaven. She was ignoring her ringing cell phone. The voice over announced, "For those times when he just doesn't get the hint." This situation sets up a contradiction. When you act in the same manner whether you want something or don't, how can anyone tell the difference? Is she hinting or just playing hard to get?

Coach Stephanie McKenzie maintains, "The self-proclaimed relationship 'experts' tell women not to call men. I asked men what would happen if she never initiated any type of conversation? Would that be endearing? How can you get to know a person when only one of you is making an effort? When I asked my cousin if she had spoken to her latest suitor, she told me, 'I called him last, so he owes me a phone call.' This is game play, but people can't play the game if they don't know the rules!"

There is the story of the racing greyhounds, the dogs that race a track chasing after a stuffed bunny. If a greyhound ever caught the fake rabbit, they would never run again. They aren't stupid; once they find out the bunny is fake, why chase it? It's a type of "been there, done that, next."

What happens after you have "caught" your partner or been "caught"? We have either heard or lived through the stories and think that once the chase is over, what else is there? A chaser, hunter, enjoys the chase, hunt; so on to the next conquest! If you begin a relationship, by either chasing or wanting to be chased, you set yourself up for either endless chases (exhausting) or one single chase (one and done, move on there is nothing to see here).

So why would anyone want to be chased? An exaggerated self-esteem, either low or high, low self-worth, high self-importance. And why would anyone want to chase? Well, for the very same reasons.

Playing hard to get goes against all the precepts I've discussed. For example, communication needs to be clear, direct and continuous. You have no one to blame but yourself for any misunderstandings that occur.

———•◆•———

27
CHAPTER

Inputs — Decisions — Outputs

I wrote this book to teach not to tell. I don't give advice; rather, I give you the tools you need to make the best decision for you, not for someone else. By knowing the "Why" and the "How," you yourself can determine the "What," that is, what you should do in relationship situations.

Many moments in our lives shape who we become. The "Inputs" begin at birth and continue through our lives. The people, places and events we are exposed to affect each of us in our own unique way. This is a cumulative process. Each item is like a piece of a puzzle, and every puzzle fits together in a different manner; even though the pieces may be similar, once they are all added together we get a unique picture, an individual. As Aristotle wisely said, "The sum of the parts is greater than the whole."

Because of our unique pasts, people, places, and events affect individuals in vastly different ways. One's personal "Inputs" tend to cloud, distort, or color his or her views of the world although not always in a negative sense. Those "Inputs" create our belief system, our values. And then our beliefs and values affect our "Outputs," the way in which we express ourselves, again clouding, distorting and coloring our actions.

Your past Inputs create Modifiers which shape your view of the world and affect your decision-making processes, both intellectual and emotional.

These Modifiers then affect the ways in which you Output, how you express yourself or communicate with others. So your Outputs

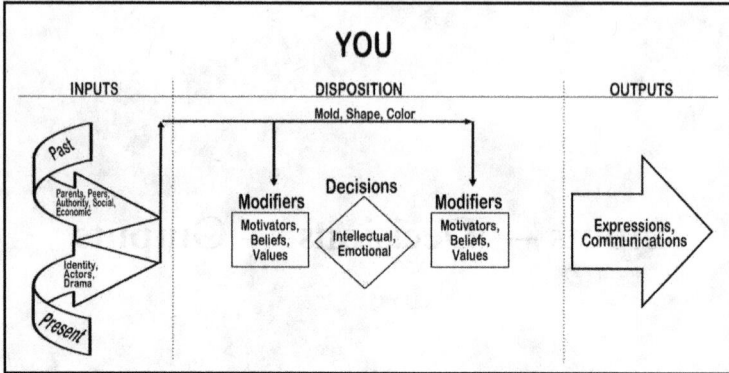

YOU

INPUTS	DISPOSITION	OUTPUTS

Mold, Shape, Color

Past

Parents, Peers, Authority, Social, Economic

Identity, Actors, Drama

Present

Modifiers
Motivators, Beliefs, Values

Decisions
Intellectual, Emotional

Modifiers
Motivators, Beliefs, Values

Expressions, Communications

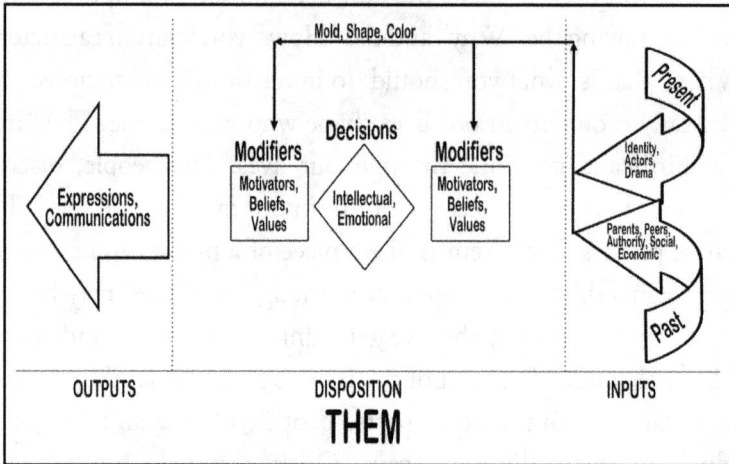

Mold, Shape, Color

Modifiers
Motivators, Beliefs, Values

Decisions
Intellectual, Emotional

Modifiers
Motivators, Beliefs, Values

Expressions, Communications

Present

Identity, Actors, Drama

Parents, Peers, Authority, Social, Economic

Past

OUTPUTS	DISPOSITION	INPUTS

THEM

GOOD TOGETHER

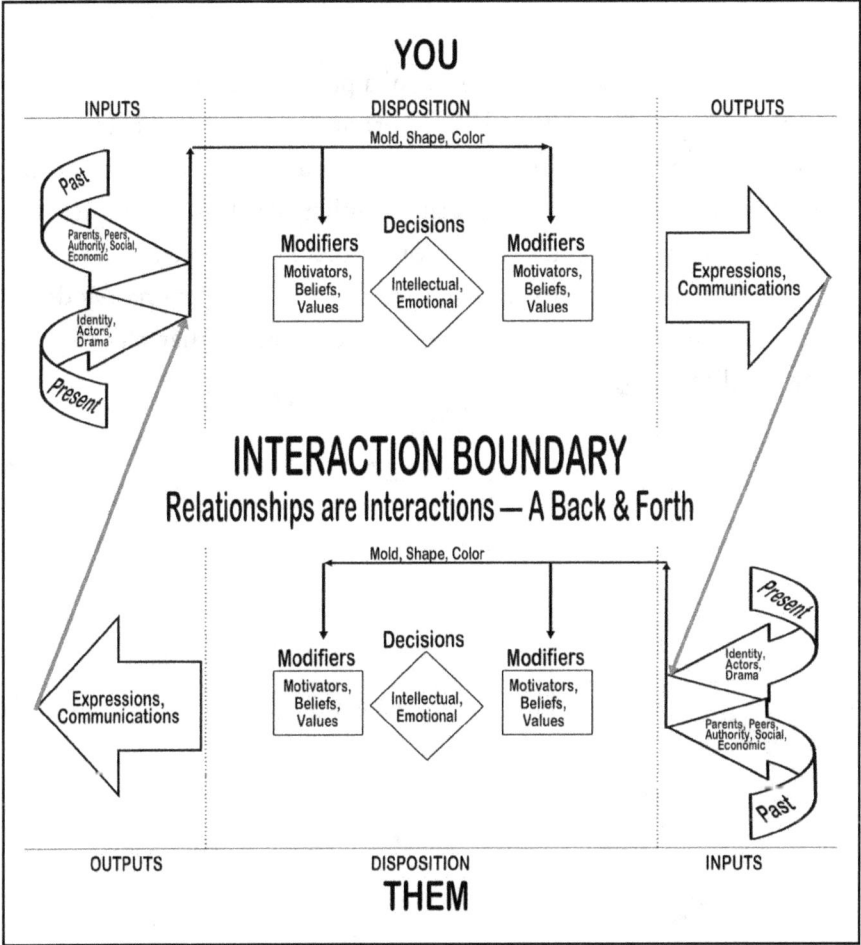

become the present Inputs to others and vice versa. This interaction or transaction of Inputs and Outputs creates our Relationships.

Puzzle Pieces

Individuals are just like pieces of a puzzle: they either fit together to create a bigger picture (Good Together) or they just don't. Even within the individual, the different pieces of a personality fit together (or don't), and when they don't, you get internal conflict which manifests itself as outputs or expressions such as depression, anxiety and stress.

All of these inputs and outputs create The Persona Model, a model of the individual, who you are, and how you got that way. (See the following diagram.)

———————————

SECTION II

Putting It All Together
The Journey Begins

28
CHAPTER

What Goes Into a Relationship?

You now have a destination, questions to ask, ways of asking, and the confidence to proceed. Next, you need to apply yourself and take the steps to embark on the journey. As you probably know, there are many people and web sites more than willing and eager to give relationship advice to anyone who will listen to or read it. By now, you should know the fact of the matter is a large amount of advice and conventional wisdom is bad or incorrect.

If these people and web sites aren't actively dispelling the bad advice, incorrect conventional wisdom, and myths, then how is it possible they will help you in your relationship? Some of them may even claim it is you who are at fault or you are too picky. They aren't able or willing to help you with your questions and concerns. In other words, they only want to tell you what they want to, not what you need to hear. They often take the easy way out, assisting those people who can easily be guided, rather than actually helping.

Relationships are continuous and cyclic. We can't ignore a relationship and expect it to continue as is. It's also true relationships have their highs and lows, so we must be prepared for the ride. Most people assume highs and lows only describe things such as excitement or passion versus reservation, boredom or worse. The fact is the highs and lows are the extremes; they occur the minority of the time; they're the exceptions, not the rule. The majority of the time is spent somewhere in between.

That in between should be spent learning, not only about others but about one's self. This, despite what you may have heard, is not hard work. Knowledge is garnered by putting forth an effort. We learn about ourselves and others through the ways we deal with various situations in life. When we stop learning new things about the other person, people, situation or ourselves, we think we know all that there is to know. We get bored. But relationships go through cycles of learning about the other person or situation, then getting used to this new information, understanding it, and then getting comfortable with it, accepting it. This cycle of learning repeats itself at varying intervals.

Of course, it is difficult to know someone, even ourselves, completely because different yet similar situations may cause greatly varying reactions. A single variation in any given circumstance may utterly change the outcome. Each person will place his own weight or value on the facets of a situation. Therefore, what seems insignificant to one person may be greatly significant to another.

We learn new things by trying new things, asking new questions, challenging ourselves and others. Depth and constancy in a relationship isn't simply the time spent. Those qualities come with stretching ourselves. For example, you may work all of your life doing the same job and only know a very small part of what is actually going on.

A friend, Bill, who manages several employees, once confided to me he was having difficulty rationalizing a raise for an employee. The problem, as he saw it, was the person had done the same thing for ten years straight, never learning new skills or acquiring new knowledge. In other words, he didn't have ten years of experience; he had one year of experience ten times over. Similarly, you could have a one-year relationship for five years because you've been doing the same thing year after year, never gaining new knowledge about yourself or your partner.

Relationships are like walking a path: if we continue to walk on, we'll see new things, be entertained and learn along the way; if, however, we stop or walk in a circle, rehashing the same old things over and over again, we won't see or learn anything new.

When you walk the path, learning new things, you may realize you must reevaluate the relationship. You need to be sure the relationship is meeting your intended and expected needs. You also must determine whether your needs, or those of the others involved in the relationship, have changed. Is the relationship you are in the relationship you want, the relationship you set out to have, or has something changed?

Relationship Success

"Success depends upon previous preparation, and without such preparation there is sure to be failure," says Confucius or, in other words, failure to plan equals planning to fail.

Relationship success begins by knowing the destination, which is the kind or type of relationship you are pursuing, what you have, what you want and what they have, what they want.

The more you know about relationships the more likely you are of attaining what you want.

- The relationship pattern: convenience or necessity, validation or appreciation, scripted, individual assertion, acceptance? Keep in mind what you have and what you want as well as what they have and what they want.
- The purpose of the relationship: pastime, healing, experimental, transitional, distraction? (What you have, what you want; what they have, what they want.)
- The duration of the relationship: short-term or long-term? (What you have, what you want; what they have, what they want.)
- The intensity or bond of the relationship: casual or serious? (What you have, what you want; what they have, what they want.)
- The objectives of the relationship: physical, emotional, intellectual? (What you have, what you want; what they have, what they want.)

- Which needs, wants, desires, will the relationship fill? (What you have, what you want; what they have, what they want.)
- The values and beliefs of the people in the relationship. (What you have, what you want; what they have, what they want.)
- The situation: business or social, family, friendship, or intimate. (What you have, what you want; what they have, what they want.)

(It is worth noting the duration and intensity are not correlated; that is, the amount of time in the relationship and how strongly you feel have very little to do with one another.)

By answering these questions fully and reasonably (no false expectations, no mutually exclusive criteria), and thereby knowing what you actually do want—and by the same token what you don't want—the problem of being "too picky" should be reduced.

Of course, simply asking questions, even the right ones, isn't enough. Oftentimes, people don't know themselves well enough to answer your questions accurately. Sometimes people are intentionally deceptive or misleading.

The fact is people don't really know who they are or what they want. For example, forty million Americans visit dating sites in any given year. Two economists and a psychologist did a study to answer two questions: How forthright are people when it comes to sharing information about themselves on their dating profiles? What information is considered most and least desirable?

They analyzed data from 20,000 profiles on a mainstream dating site, half in San Diego and half in Boston. The results were startling if not surprising.

- People claimed to be richer, taller, skinnier, better looking than the average person;

- 4% claimed to earn over $200k a year, compared to less than 1% of internet users;
- Both males and females reported to be about an inch taller than the national average;
- Men reported their weight at about the national average, but women reported being 20 pounds lighter than the national average;
  72% of women claimed "above average" looks with 24% claiming "very good looks;"
- 68% of men claimed above average looks and 19% "very good looking;"
- Only 1% claimed to be of "less than average looks;"
- 28% of women said they were blonde, which is far beyond the national average.
- Some answers were "bracingly honest":
- 7% of men reported they were married, with a significant a number reporting "happily married;"
- Of the 243 "happily married" men, only 12 did not post a photo of themselves.

(By the way, the surest way to fail on a dating website is not to post a photo of yourself. A man who does not post a photo gets only 60% of the emails, a woman who does not post a photo gets 24% of the emails. The odds aren't great even if you do post a photo: 56% of men who posted ads didn't get a single email; 21% of women didn't get a single email.)

Some interesting facts, again not surprising, came out of the study:

- Men who say they want a long-term relationship do better than those who say they want an occasional lover;
- Women who say they want an occasional lover do great;
- For men, a woman's looks are most important;
- For women, a man's income is most important. The richer a man is, the more emails he receives;
- For men, a woman's income is a bell-curve. Men do

not want a low-income woman, but they don't want a very high income woman either;

- Women are eager to date fire fighters, military, policemen, lawyers, doctors and avoid manufacturing workers;
- For men, being short is a big disadvantage; for women, being overweight is a big disadvantage;
- For men, having red hair, curly hair, or being bald with a fringe is bad, but a shaved head is fine;
- For women, having salt and pepper hair is a disadvantage, being blonde is an advantage.

Race preferences indicated by users were usually "the same as mine" or "doesn't matter." However, white men who said race didn't matter sent 90% of their emails to white women, and white women who said race didn't matter sent 97% of their emails to white men. Did they only say it didn't matter in order to appear open-minded?

So what does it mean to match someone on values or beliefs? First, only those values pertinent to the type of relationship need to be explored. Is it necessary to know the political preferences in a convenience relationship? It may not be. Second, even in intimate relationships, the likelihood you will match on every value is not realistic or reasonable. In addition, the strength of your beliefs or values may not be exactly identical. Of course, the more similarities, and the stronger, the better, but how much is enough?

The paradox is in order to understand relationship success fully, we must explore some of the reasons for relationship failures.

Oftentimes, people begin a relationship with a relationship type they think they want in their mind. Then they find a person, or people, they want in that particular relationship and proceed to force them together. But we can't force fit a person, or people, into our specific expectation of a relationship.

For example, you may want to be friends with someone, but if the other person won't cooperate, if he or she doesn't act like or treat you like a friend the way you want to be treated, then you will not achieve a friendship relationship.

It takes all the parties in a relationship to act in a way others will accept. This requires people in the relationship to know what is expected from them and the relationship. Often, we don't see our part or contribution in the shaping of the relationship; instead, we want simply to be the recipients of the benefits of the relationship. All relationships have an implied contract: you are who you portray yourself to be, and you will remain true to yourself.

Where Have All the Good Ones Gone?

You might not know a good one if he or she were standing right in front of you. You either don't know what to look for or you want what does not actually exist. If you want what doesn't exist, then you have to come to the realization you are not one of the good ones. You haven't put in the effort to either get, or deserve, one of them.

A better question might be, "Why would one of the good ones want me?" It isn't that they don't exist; it isn't about them at all. It is all about you.

Now it isn't a hard and fast or binding contract, and of course it can accommodate for items outside of your control; however, there are limits to what will and what won't be accepted. For example, one contract issue is a person's appearance. Basically, the contract says that for the most part I like you the way you are; if I didn't, I wouldn't, shouldn't, have pursued a relationship with you in the first place. We don't ask each other to weigh in each day, and we aren't capable of estimating an individual's weight to within more than just a few pounds. In addition, generally, a few pounds one way or the other is offset by many of the other attributes we find appealing and attractive about the other person. However, there may come a time when you are not the person you used to be.

Here's an example from my experience: I work out, lift weights daily, rollerblade regularly, and eat reasonably. I started dating a woman, and I have to believe my physical appearance was appealing, at least in part, but almost immediately she told me I was working out too much. She wanted to spend more time with me. Now anyone who works out knows a consistent schedule is key to consistent results and motivation to keep working out. However, following bad advice, and in the interest of the relationship, I compromised and worked out less often.

At the same time, as is common in new relationships, we began eating out regularly.

She initially joined me in rollerblading, but that didn't last, and I was asked to find something else we could do together. As time went by, I gained one pound after another until I had gained forty pounds and grown four pant sizes.

Needless to say, the relationship ended, and although she never actually said so, I know I wasn't the person she had started dating. I had broken the contract. What was worse was I had lost my self. At the end of the relationship, I was devastated because I didn't have me to hang on to. After that, I started rollerblading again, eating healthy, and working out, weight lifting. I have lost all forty pounds and four pant sizes. I feel good about me physically, emotionally and mentally.

Maybe my relationship with this woman was the result of "relationship starvation." If you are in the desert and starving, you'll likely accept food you might otherwise find distasteful. The same can be said of relationships, both business and social. If you don't have a job and you're in need of one, you'll likely accept work you otherwise wouldn't. If you feel you need a relationship, you may accept a "better than nothing" or a "Mr. / Ms. Right Now" instead of "Mr. / Ms. Right."

But once you have your footing and have reestablished your self-esteem and confidence, you may feel you can do better, find a better job, a better partner.

Sitting at Home

Speed dating promises to weed out the undesirables and match you with someone who attracts you in the first few seconds, and those are seconds, studies suggest, that matter the most. Whether the process works well is dubious, but in the interests of coming at relationship decisions from all angles, allow me to share the following information.

Researchers studied the effects of an individual being approached versus the prospects of one approaching. When they reversed the roles of the men and women, that is, women approached men, they found women were much more receptive to second dates with more of the men.

However, when women go to a function and sit passively by waiting to be approached, they rarely are. The lesson here is anything worth getting is worth going after. The surface mentality of many women and men can be exposed by describing a cartoon I once saw: a young boy and girl stand next to one another. The boy pulls down his pants and says, "I have one of these." The girl responds by pulling up her dress and saying, "Well, I have one of these, and with one of these I can get as many of those as I want!"

If this were truly the case, then there would be no single, lonely, women in the world. Any women could have any man.

Now for the truth. You can only get those people who are around you. You aren't likely to get a movie star, star athlete, or billionaire if you don't run in their circles. You can't get those people who don't present themselves to you. If the person you're eyeing across the room doesn't approach you, and you don't approach him or her, you won't meet. You won't get hired by every company you interview with; you won't hit it off with every person you come in contact with. In some cases, they won't be drawn to you, and in other cases you won't be drawn to them.

We all know you won't find the career you want by sitting at home. You must be involved, even take charge, of your situation. The same is true of intimate relationships.

So what is a successful relationship? Coach Stephanie McKenzie says, "I would say one where fundamentally the people are able to connect in a mutually beneficial and pleasing way, despite the challenges of their day to day lives. But then again it's successful if two people find out they don't need to be together."

29
CHAPTER

Myth —You Deserve a Relationship

Relationships and happiness are earned: they require time, effort, and sacrifice. Just as you don't deserve a raise just for showing up to work every day, you don't deserve a relationship; you have to earn it. Many people feel they are entitled to a relationship, and happiness, just for showing up. But that feeling confuses deserving with entitlement.

Along the same lines is the belief you'll "find a relationship when you aren't really looking for one." No. If you aren't looking, you could very well not notice the great relationship right in front of your face. You don't get a job by not looking, at least not the job you want; maybe you get the job that wants you.

You Can't Have It All

Being "picky" stems from unrealistic expectations, which are rooted in bad advice, such as "You can have it all." I'm sorry to tell you that you cannot have it all, first, not all at once, and second, you don't even want it all. "Be careful what you wish for."

You find a relationship, business or social, when you are open and available for a relationship and when you earn it. If it were true that "you find a relationship when you aren't looking for one," we would have to ask, "Who are the very people who aren't looking for relationships?" The answer is those who already have, or are in, relationships. Therefore, that statement is justifying either cheating or relationship hopping.

But you won't find one when you are on the prowl or actively hunting your prey because being overly aggressive and trying to force fit a relationship gives an air of desperation. People are drawn to confidence not despair; there is a difference between looking for, and begging for, a relationship.

A better way of going about finding a relationship is to be both comfortable with ourselves and our situations, and appear open to the possibilities a new relationship offers.

———◆◆◆———

30

Relationship Stages

Statistics indicate many relationships run their course in approximately four years, not the seven year itch you've heard so much about. Interestingly, this four-year pattern of enthusiasm, coming together, complacency, and then moving apart, shows up in other areas. Car loans, getting through high school, gaining a college degree, presidential terms are all four year stretches.

I changed work duties every three to four years while staying at the same company, changes which kept boredom at bay. It's as if our human attention has a "natural" span. Is it simply coincidence these important milestones occur every four years or have people, through observation, found this pattern to be most useful?

> ## Relationship Building Stages
>
> **Initiation:** first impressions, light conversation, surveying.
> **Exploration:** finding common ground.
> **Intensification:** test and foster relationship.
> **Integration:** merging, loyalty to the relationship.
> **Bonding:** commitment to the world.

We get excited about something new, all the possibilities, and we set high expectations for what things are going to be like. As time passes, things settle into a routine and get stale. Maybe the novelty wears off or maybe the relationship is nothing like we imagined.

Similar stages occur in all these events. In the beginning of a personal relationship, there is the phase of coming together, a building of intensity.

Initiation: this is where first impressions are made. Often physical factors play a role in this stage, such as clothing, perfumes or colognes, hair styles, and overall appearance. People often want to portray themselves as easy to talk to, friendly, and open to discussion. This stage does not include deep revealing conversations but rather light conversation meant to survey the possibility of a closer personal relationship.

Exploration: in this stage of the relationship, people attempt to find some common ground between each other's lives such as interests and hobbies. This stage is also referred to as the probing stage, because each person probes the other for information that would allow them to further the social connection between them. Many relationships end here, never developing to anything more than a mere acquaintance.

Intensification: this stage also tests the potential of the relationship with varying degrees of self-disclosure to see if that trait will be reciprocated and to test the impressions one is making. In the intensifying stage of the Relationship Development Model, relationships grow and self-disclosure becomes more apparent and deep. People find many different ways to foster their relationships in order to stimulate relational development. Methods include giving gifts, asking for a romantic relationship commitment or expressing affection both verbally and nonverbally. Of course, there are no set guidelines for every relationship in the intensifying stage. Every relationship possesses unique characteristics making it difficult for the Relationship Development Model to predict accurately if those efforts to further the relationship will succeed or fail. Partners in some relationships may "test the waters" to see if particular advances are welcomed or frowned upon. These "secret" tests are intended to test the intensity of a relationship. They can include presenting the other person as a girlfriend or boyfriend (presentation) to others or seeing if the relationship lasts when a temporary physical separation occurs between the two people. Others will openly engage in a declaration to the other of their intent to be exclusive in some fashion.

Integration: this is where people begin to merge and their loyalty to the relationship becomes apparent. In friendships, separate groups are introduced to each other and possibly combined. In intimate relationships, family are brought into and included in the relationship.

Bonding: in this stage, the commitment of the relationship is communicated to the rest of the world, typically by means of significant societal actions such as marriage or living together.

However, if the relationship is not tended to properly, and little or no maintenance is performed, it will enter the phase of moving apart, a waning of intensity. These stages will likely follow:

Differentiation: differences are exploited instead of the commonalities of the exploration and intensifying stages. The momentum of the "work together" attitude quickly shifts directions and becomes more individualistic. Some may describe feelings of being held down and become resentful of their commitment to their partner.

Circumscription: the primary focus of the relationship shifts from differences to setting limits and boundaries on communication between people. The communication becomes shallower and the range of topics significantly declines. Partners may fear discussing deep topics because of the threat of a conflict, leading to less communication altogether.

Stagnation: this stage builds off many of the problems of the circumscribing stage. Communication becomes more limited and less frequent. Relationships in this stage do not grow or progress but rather invoke a feeling of "nothing changes."

Avoidance: here, the limited communication moves to a physical level. Partners may avoid each other altogether, desiring separation from one another.

Termination: the relationship stops completely.

Let's note, however, the coming apart stages are not necessarily negative. Sometimes, it is healthy for two people to terminate their relationship in the interest of personal aspirations and well-being.

These stages cannot accurately describe all relationships because each relationship moves at a different speed and is affected by the personalities and communication abilities of the people involved. However, by combining the four year time frame and the stages, we may be able, to some degree, to determine what to expect and approximately when to expect it.

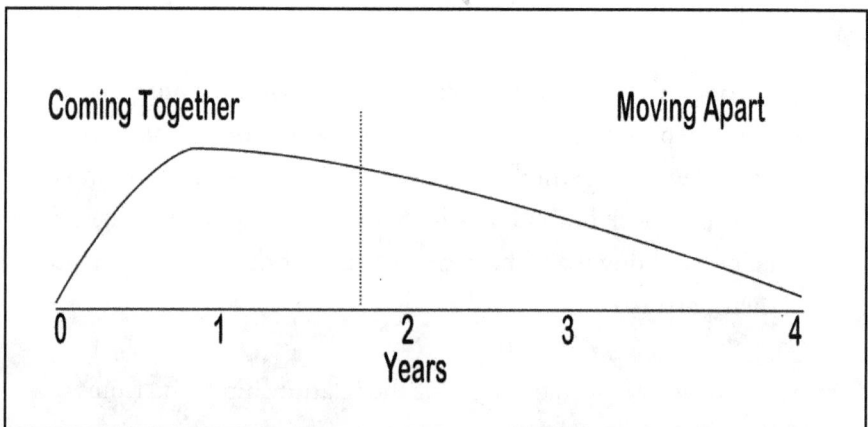

(This is Knapp's Relational Development Model. I have altered some of the stage names to what I believe more accurately reflects events and emotions.)

Things begin hot and heavy, they then settle down into a moderate burn. If the fire starts to diminish, we harken back to when it burned bright, in other words we are withdrawing from the bank of past emotions. This is one of the reasons that we may stay past the point of the fire going cold, and the moving apart becomes mired in what could have, should have, been.

Humans may not be so different from their nearest relation: even monkeys get tired of their mates at the three to four year mark. In a study of monkey mating, it was discovered the male monkeys had to be replaced on a three-year cycle because the females would lose interest at that point, a kind of human reaction: "Been there, done that." Humans, however, having an emotional and intellectual bond, have the ability to connect on a number of different ideas and levels and to differing degrees. Monkeys don't: one monkey doesn't value the other monkey's desire to save the rainforest.

———•◆•———

31
CHAPTER

Relationship Styles

At each stage in a relationship you learn more about each other. Either or both of the emotional and intellectual may affect the perception of the physical: the more you like someone the more attractive they become in your eyes and vice versa.

One's ideals, beliefs, values or convictions are inherently tied to both emotions and intellect; therefore, values are not clearly separable from emotions or intellect.

When a woman asks me, "Do these pants make my butt look big?" I find it difficult to answer. I don't see her simply physically, even though this may be originally what I found appealing. I don't see her through those eyes because our connection is clouding my view. She must understand I'm not one of her friends. She's talking to the person who wants to rip those pants off with his teeth; she must realize she just gave me permission to check out her butt. Wait, did you say something to me? I got distracted.

When I talk about style, I'm referring to the appeal and attraction of the relationship. Relationships can be simple, with an attraction that is either physical, emotional, intellectual, or of ideals. Or they may be more complex, having a combination of any or all of these elements, and to varying degrees. The *style* of the relationship associates closely with the *purpose* of the relationship. What this means is the purpose of the relationship may be dependent on the elements of appeal and attraction.

For example, if the purpose of the relationship is strictly one of pastime, then it may also be simply, and singularly, physical, emotional, intellectual, or one of ideals. If the purpose of the relationship is healing, then the style may be emotional and a sharing of ideals. If the relationship is mainly convenience, it may proceed on physical grounds alone.

———•◦•———

32
CHAPTER

Relationship Synchronicity

What is music and what is noise? What is the difference?

The technical, and correct, answer is they are both sound. Some people, when in an elevator, will think the sounds piped in are "white noise." Clearly, though, the sound is intentional, it was composed, and intended to be enjoyed, maybe not by all but at least by some. On the other hand, a store owner may hear the ring of the cash drawer as it opens and exclaim, "That's music to my ears," even though it isn't composed or meant to be enjoyed as music. Music, then, is what we "want" to hear, whereas noise is what we "don't want" to hear. It is strictly individual.

So what is work, and what is play or fun?

You should already know the answer. Both work and play are actually effort, the difference being fun is the effort "you want" to exert, whereas work is the effort that "other people want you" to exert. As Confucius said, "Choose a job that you love, and you will never have to work a day in your life."

Don't let anyone tell you that relationships are "hard work." (More on this later.) However, people seem to believe that when they find a person they click with, it will be all smooth sailing from then on. These are both extreme viewpoints, neither of which is based in reality. The truth lies somewhere in the middle, which is "effort." Remember, even fun is effort. The same could be said about finding a job or a relationship: you need to expend "effort." Neither saying it's "hard work" nor it will take "no work" is reasonable or realistic. People think there should be no disagreements or no discontent or the disagreements should all be minor, nothing to be concerned about.

Now let's consider the harsh reality.

There are two sides to every relationship; otherwise it wouldn't be a relationship. Let's suppose, for simplicity, you want to spend time in your new relationship. Of course, you can't spend all of your time in the relationship. By the same token, the other person in the relationship will want to spend time in the new relationship, yet neither can they spend all of their time in the relationship. When the two of you want to be together, everything is great; even when you both can't be together, at least the two of you are in agreement.

However, what happens when one of the two of you wants to spend time together, but the other person cannot spend time with you. You likely imagine these times will be few and far between, and so this is insignificant. Let's assume you want to spend five out of seven days a week with them, and they, too, want to spend five out of seven days a week with you. Wonderful. You're a perfect match! Hold on, now, because the days may not align just the way you imagine.

You	Them	Total
Want to spend time together (5 days)	Want to spend time together (5 days)	Combined (3.5 days)
Want to spend time together (5 days)	Need time apart (2 days)	Combined (1.5 days)
Need time apart (2 days)	Want to spent time together (5 days)	Combined (1.5 days)
Need time apart (2 days)	Need time apart (2 days)	Combined (0.5 day)

As you can see, you'll both agree to spend time together 3.5 days a week because one of the two of you won't be able to get together, that is, you'll be out of synch with each other, a total of three days a week, and you'll both agree to spend time apart just a half a day per week.

What this means is you aren't as synchronous as you may think. This isn't a *problem*—this is just the fact that two different people can't, and don't, always have the same needs, goals, availability. It also means that from time to time, even though you don't feel like it, you need to push yourself to make time for one another.

Your Relationship Account

A relationship is like a bank account. In the beginning of the relationship you're putting money in the account hand over fist. At some point, you forget to deposit because you get complacent and then you're only withdrawing. As long as you're putting money back in, your balance won't get into negatives. But if you only withdraw, at some point you will start bouncing checks, and the account will be closed.

I had explained this concept of people not always being on the same page at the same time to a business colleague. Her attitude was it wasn't a problem for her and her husband because they scheduled time together in the evenings and on weekends. Weeks later, she received a phone call from her husband during a full-day meeting. He asked if she could meet him for lunch, and I noticed that his questioning seemed persistent. She was upset about the call, that he had called at all which was not like him and that he'd been reluctant to hear her decline the invitation. Later, I felt compelled to remind her of the reality of synchronicity. I told her I felt he was informing her, although not clearly and not directly, that he wanted to spend quality time with her and her alone, as a couple.

We can't control or schedule our wants, needs, cravings, or desires; they come when they come. This isn't to say we must drop what we are doing and run to each other's side whenever we snap our fingers, or they request, any more than we should repress, deny, or withhold our affections from one another. That would actually be detrimental.

Instead, we should acknowledge and capture our feelings, making sure they are put to good use. What my colleague might have done is acknowledge her appreciation for his affections and reassure him they would not go to waste, making sure to spend quality time with him in a reasonable amount of time, while conjuring and reigniting his pressing desires.

You have heard the phrase "The only constant is change." Relationships are no different. People in a relationship—business or personal—never expect it will change, and, as a consequence of this thinking, they don't plan for the future of the relationship. At the same time, most will say they want the relationship to grow. But growing, in fact, necessitates change.

Relationships begin with varying degrees of satisfaction. Some start slowly and increase in satisfaction, some start intensely and manage to stay that way, and others burn out over time. Things can either get better, stay the same, or get worse. If the relationship is good—moods, occurrences are positive—then getting better or staying the same is a beneficial situation; however, if things are bad, then staying the same or getting worse is an unlucky situation.

Progress requires change: every progression requires a transition from the here and now to the there and then. Risk and effort are associated with every change or transition. There is the risk of either losing what we have, that is the transition or relationship progresses to a worse situation, or there is the risk of our investments going unrewarded, which means staying the same or getting worse.

The paradox is even to keep a good relationship staying the same—that is, staying good—requires some effort.

The amount of risk, the effort, and the value of the reward are central to our goal of satisfaction. Satisfaction, being highly desirable and rather rare, is high risk because it's what you want, or what you're trying to attain; on the other hand, un-satisfaction, being highly undesirable and rather abundant, constitutes a low risk.

For clarity, un-satisfaction is not dissatisfaction, which is actual discontent or displeasure. Un-satisfaction is merely ambivalence. As relationships progress, one of three things may occur: the relationship may "improve," "remain the same" (stagnate), or "diminish." As the relationship progresses, and as your feelings or situations change, you will need to choose either to stay or leave. The fact is, though, people usually reverse the cause and effect. They use the "stay or leave" criteria to determine their fate regardless of the progression. Then they either accept the state of the relationship as it is, try to fix the broken relationship or languish in misery.

For example, we may begin with a satisfactory relationship and transition to staying in the relationship.

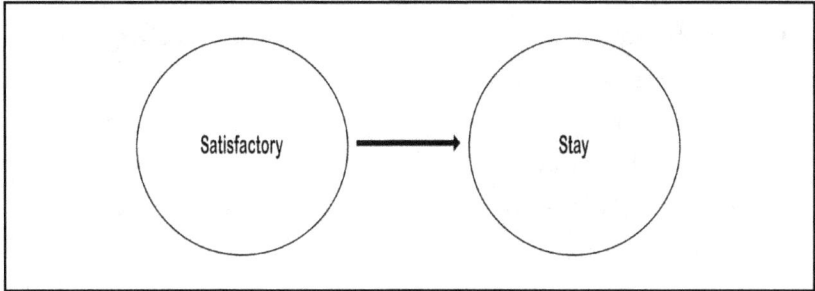

The risk is high, as you are risking continued satisfaction. The effort is low, but not nonexistent. There is no such thing as satisfaction without any effort because even if you have satisfaction now, you will need to invest effort simply to keep the momentum. Just as it takes a certain amount of gasoline (effort) to get a car moving from a complete stop to the desired speed, so once the car is moving, it requires less energy to keep it at speed. However, it does require energy. There is no free ride. Satisfaction today in no way guarantees satisfaction tomorrow. Another analogy exists between keeping relationships going and putting money in the bank: investing and not living from pay check to pay check allows you some breathing room and the occasional vacation without worrying about bounced checks. So it is with relationships: some effort or good will invested in a relationship today can be drawn on tomorrow if need be. The effort actually does not, and should not, need to be a constant one.

Suppose you are in a satisfactory relationship and you transition to leaving the relationship. The risk is high and the effort is likely also high.

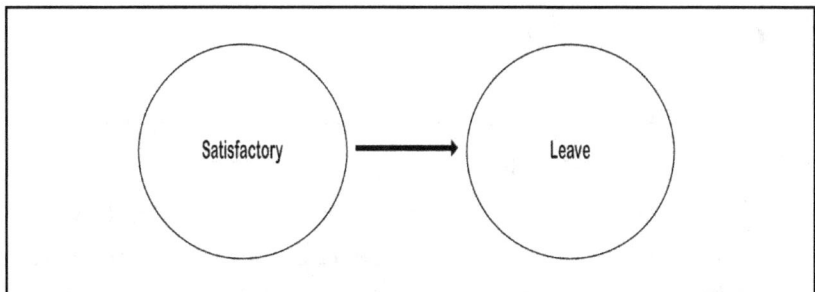

On the surface, this scenario seems unlikely, even absurd, but it may be much more common than most people realize, especially when we consider conflicting priorities around work or families. Suppose you really enjoy your job, but your partner gets a job in a different state; you may have to leave a satisfying relationship, business or social, even though you'd rather not. One myth about relationship progression is marital satisfaction increases after having children. In fact, it consistently plummets after a couple first has children, then rebounds. In other words, some changes to a good, healthy relationship, which are meant to be additive, may actually cause stress and tax the original, base relationship. Therein lies the risk to the relationship.

In life's situations, we often have to choose between two competing items, giving up one satisfaction for another. For example, think of the choices the characters have to make in the movie *Casablanca*. Rick and Ilsa are in love, but Ilsa is married to Victor, a key player leading the resistance against the Nazis. Ilsa is willing to leave her husband for Rick; but Rick, knowing the loss would crush Victor and thereby cripple the resistance and cost countless lives, pushes Ilsa away, almost forcing her to stay with Victor. It's the ultimate self-sacrifice for both.

Although you and I may never find ourselves in that particular position, we may, from time to time, do what is best for someone else although it goes against our own satisfaction.

Let us say we are in an unsatisfactory relationship, and we transition to leaving.

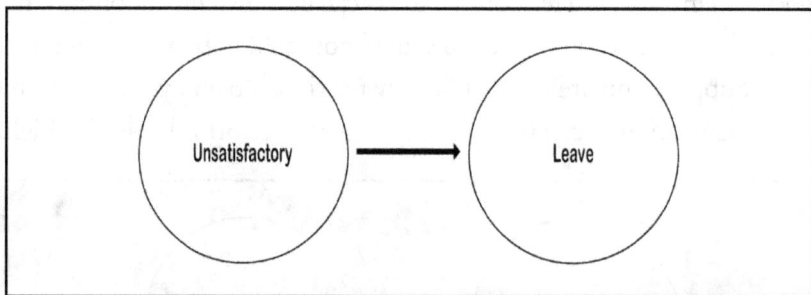

Your risk, which is low, is your un-satisfaction. Your effort is expended not in continuing the relationship, but in leaving the relationship. It takes courage and confidence to face the unknown, which is high risk and takes great effort.

Leaving a relationship can be a difficult decision. People have good reasons and inferior reasons to abandon a relationship. Sometimes a person leaves because he or she is expending effort in an attempt to find a better relationship. Leaving a relationship to improve your relationship with yourself is reasonable and will likely improve your chances at a future relationship. Quitting a relationship which is not meeting your needs, so long as those needs and expectations are well understood and are reasonable is commendable. However, leaving one relationship, when you don't know what you want, in search of another relationship in the hopes it will fill a void is irrational and unreasonable. Jumping from one relationship to the next with no end in sight likely signals either lack of knowledge of self or others, unrealistic expectations or both. You will likely find only more of the same, feelings of emptiness and despair.

By the same token, leaving a relationship without allowing the other party an opportunity to right the wrongs or address the issues is running

It's All About Respect

My friend Eric and I have some different, even opposite, opinions and beliefs, some of which are significant, dealing with issues defining us as individuals. So how do two very different people not only coexist but get along well together?

It is a matter of respect.

Respect is defined as due regard, consideration, and concern for the feelings, wishes, rights, or traditions of others. I would add that so long as those feelings are, in turn, respectful of others, that they do not infringe on the rights of others, and are in no way against the consent of others, or are not forceful, coercive, intimidating, or maliciously manipulative of others, one maintains respect.

People mistakenly believe respect is agreement; but the highest form of respect is that which is given in the face of disagreement. It is easy to respect those with whom you agree, but it is a great deal more difficult, and honorable, to respect those with whom you disagree. Respect is understanding the rights of others to have their own personal views, perspectives and beliefs which differ from your own.

Some of the key factors to Eric's and my getting along are that we never force our beliefs on the other person. When-

Continued on Page 180

Continued from Page 179

ever we discuss topics upon which we do not see eye to eye, we make clear from the outset our opinions are our own: they are personal and are by no means universal. Therefore, it is understood the other person is not only free to his own beliefs, but he has every right to his own beliefs. We understand and accept our beliefs have been shaped by our personal journeys through life. Because we have not lived the same life, we can never have the exact beliefs. We admire each other for having beliefs and sharing those beliefs. In order for us to grow, we must be willing to share our beliefs and listen to the beliefs of others.

For me, the respect is more important than the beliefs themselves. As long as the respect is mutual, it is honored.

Respect from someone who differs from you is more obvious than the respect of someone who agrees with you. As such, the respect of seeming opposites appears to be more valuable.

away. It is a waste of the effort invested in the relationship up to that point. People won't always see eye to eye, but avoiding the issues and abandoning a relationship at the first, or slightest, sign of trouble means never settling down into a stable relationship again. Unfortunately, you can expect more of the same: fleeing from one relationship to the next with no end in sight.

You might be asking, how much effort is enough or when is the correct time to leave a relationship?

Limits and boundaries are terms of self-respect. Others won't respect you if you don't respect yourself. If you know what you need and want— that is, you have clear limits or boundaries for yourself—and your expectations are reasonable, then you have to decide whether those expectations are being met. Your boundaries are not threats to the other party; the other party doesn't even need to know what the limits are. They are for your own peace of mind; they are your own internal protection mechanism.

However, if you haven't set your own limits, then you can't rightfully say the other party has taken advantage of you by over stepping the boundaries that don't exist.

Knowing the reasons you're leaving a relationship and feeling confident those reasons are sensible and well-founded are the key differentiators between feeling the decision to leave was the correct one or a feeling of uncertainty and dread.

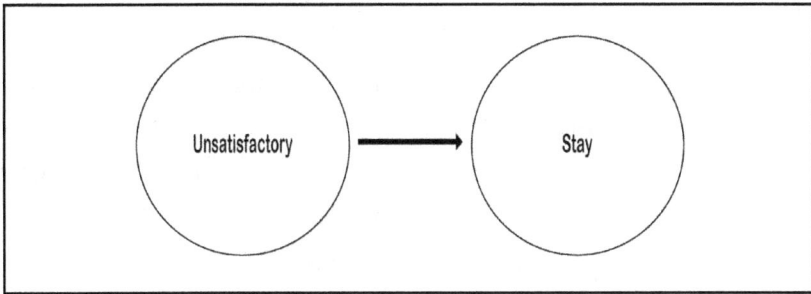

In the case of an unsatisfactory relationship and the choice to stay, your risk is your un-satisfaction, which is low. The effort depends on if you choose to improve your situation or simply bear it.

Just as continued satisfaction is not guaranteed in a satisfactory relationship, it isn't a guarantee that being unsatisfied will be the outcome of a relationship that is not satisfactory. In other words, the situation doesn't necessarily have to remain unsatisfactory. It is, however, the most likely, even expected, outcome of the relationship because it takes a lot less effort to remain unsatisfied than it does to remain satisfied.

"Earned" Respect

Many people believe that "Respect is Earned." My position is "Disrespect is Earned." The default, or normal starting position, should always be one of respect, and from that point on people can either earn, through their own actions, disrespect or greater respect. And remember, you are a reflection of yourself. In other words, if you don't respect yourself, you can't respect others and vice versa.

You may have your reasons for staying in an unsatisfactory relationship: perhaps you desire to salvage or repair the relationship. This will take a lot of effort. You are attempting to right the wrongs and get the relationship back on track, to the way things used to be. This is change: from one set of circumstances to another. But, remember, any effort to change must involve all parties and entice all parties to participate in change. No one of the parties can go on indefinitely expending great amounts of effort with no, or little, reciprocation.

Three Factors of Relationship Satisfaction

Knowledge: The more you know about how to define a relationship, about yourself, about others and about the ways people interact in various relationships, the more prepared you are to be in a relationship. As the old saying goes, "To be forewarned is to be forearmed."

Expectations: The more reasonable your expectations and the more you respect the expectations of others, the more likely you are to achieve your desired, mutual outcome.

Investment: The more both of you invest in the relationship, and in each other, the greater the bonds and connections between you. This is a mutual investment, a balanced investment, which is not to say the same type of investment. But it is not one-sided. This type of investment is reciprocal, so it progresses gradually, back and forth.

If the effort you are putting into the relationship pays no dividends, then the effort is not worth the reward; what you get in return isn't worth the pain and suffering. Yes, you may have some sunny days or occasional gains, but the cost is so great there isn't anything left in the bank.

Consider why you should stay. Perhaps you have no real purpose other than fear of change or the fear of being alone. This is a relationship where simply existing in the relationship is "hard work," so much so that you stop working, you stop making an effort. The ripple effect occurs: if you aren't making an effort, then nothing will change. This situation is analogous to a job you would rather not do: you hate getting up in the morning and going to the same old job doing the same old thing, but you continue because you don't know what else to do.

Another situation consists of the unsatisfactory relationship with the choice of both staying and leaving.

Your risk is both your un-satisfaction which registers low and your satisfaction which is high. The effort is highly intense because it is doubled; you actually exist in two different relationships at the same time. You're staying physically and leaving emotionally. You supplement or fill the void of something missing in one relationship with an entirely different relationship. In the short term, you are probably looking for something else altogether. In the long term, there is some, but not complete, satisfaction with the new relationship, and some, but not complete, un-satisfaction with the original relationship. In intimate relationships, this stay/leave is characterized as cheating. In business, it may be job hunting or using on the job time to do non-work related projects. If you use the time and resources of one job while doing another job, you're perceived as stealing.

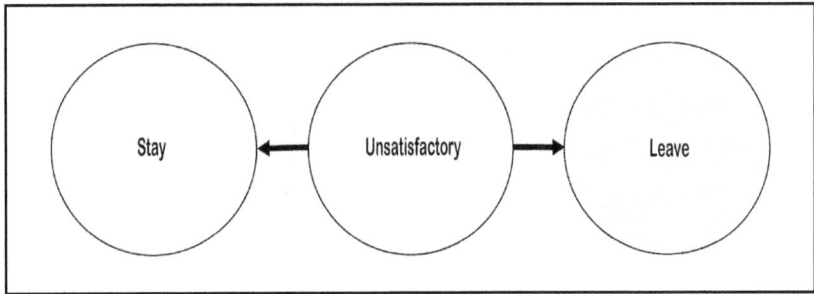

Why do people stay/leave? They may not be confident they can find another relationship which can take the place of the present one. A person may be experiencing a fear of loss, low self-esteem, a sense of undeserving, or the avoidance of some issue. It may be an attempt to replace what one has while avoiding any lapse, or gap, in benefits.

It may look like the best of both worlds, but it only applies to you. As this situation benefits you and only you, the stay/leave scenario is entirely selfish, self-centered.

People often neglect to think about how relationships progress or change over time. For that reason, you must reassess your relationships and your situations periodically in order to reverse the sequence of simply choosing whether to "Stay" or whether "to Leave" regardless of the situation, and to determine if the situation warrants you to "Stay" or to "Leave."

33
CHAPTER

"Trust Me!"

Never trust a person who has to tell you to trust them.

Trust is neither positive nor negative. If I say I trust you will steal from me, that isn't a positive trust. Substitute the word "believe" for the word "trust." So why do we believe one thing and not another? Past experience. You believe or trust someone because he or she has proven himself/herself in the same or similar situation. When we say we don't know if we can trust someone, what we are really saying is we don't have enough information to feel comfortable predicting an outcome. It isn't that we trust negatively. We cannot trust what we do not know. Trust is "past performance influencing future expectations."

Trust is earned, gradually over time, and built on previously earned trust. The phrase "Actions speak louder than words" is an example of our coming to trust: when the actions match the words there is no greater foundation for trust.

So how can we build increasing and measure decreasing trust? Trust requires action, not passivity. You have to pay attention to the words and actions of the people in the relationship. Don't blindly, repeatedly, give people the benefit of the doubt; don't give it away freely or cheaply. Make people earn your trust.

Building Trust

First, you need to determine how important an issue is to you. If your beloved wrecks your car because he or she has been drinking, is that important? If your beloved loses your credit card? If he or she cheats at poker? Once we decide an issue is of importance, we need to make all those involved aware of the status of it. "I don't trust you to drive my car when you drink." "We can replace the credit card." "What, you cheat at cards?" Of course, if it isn't important, then forget it. In either case, don't carry it around with you, allowing it to fester and grow. Keep in mind the relative importance, given any other, pertinent, issues; don't focus on this item singularly. Don't make a mountain out of a molehill because it is all you can see. Take a step back and view the situation as a whole. Then you can decide for yourself what the solution to the issue could be, not should be.

For relationships, the solution to some trust issues may be the end of the relationship. Determine how often the trust has been either broken or confirmed. This may indicate a pattern, either positive or negative, which creates expectations, both yours and theirs. Notice how recently a similar occurrence took place. When was the last time he wrecked your car after drinking? This may be a clue to you that a more vigilant awareness on your part is necessary.

You'll need to set limits on how you're going to act and react. You'll need to set real boundaries you are willing to maintain in resolving the issue. For example, how many times are you going to try doing something—loaning him your car—or how long will you allow the situation to persist—her cheating on you?

What are you willing to accept as a change? No more drinking? No more driving? You can apply a process to come up with resolutions, but people rarely take the time to learn about or apply the process. Then they wonder why a relationship blows up in their faces and they didn't know what was going on. Well, they weren't paying attention. They never set any real limits of what to do, how long to do it, what to expect, or what they were willing to accept.

In a case in which someone deceives you, you might be able to let it go the first time. Until it happens again and again. Recently, I talked to a loving, mature woman who had been in a relationship for about three years. From the very beginning, she had made it clear to her partner she did not date married men, to which statement he assured her he was not married. (The fact she was uneasy about him and his situation should have raised questions in her mind.) He had told her he was previously married. After three years, she apprehensively went online to research his background through public records of marriage and divorce. She told me she found a record of his marriage license; however, there was no record of his divorce. Unhappy and fearful, she confronted him with this information. He raged and stormed and claimed she was in the wrong, having searched incorrectly, yet he never provided the proof himself. Finally, she found out through a mutual acquaintance he was indeed still legally married. To her credit, devastated by his lies, she promptly ended the relationship.

She asked me how she could ever trust other men and what she should have done differently. The problem was the person she didn't trust was herself. She didn't trust her own instincts or better judgment. She had seen all of the warning signs, yet she never followed through with them. She suspected a problem, but she turned a blind eye, choosing to give trust where none had been earned. She chose to put the relationship before her own self-interest.

At some point, you may reach a breaking point where a situation is no longer acceptable, and you have to let the relationship go.

A deception or offense may be seen as a personal attack, which may set off a situation of retribution, which may be like for like, or an escalating of attacks. However, this tit-for-tat mentality will satisfy you only about half the time and, eventually, the relationship settles into a back and forth cycle. There is no real resolution. You will have to decide whether you are going to let go of the deception or the relationship.

Someone has to be strong enough and mature enough to restrain himself or herself from further indignation. Someone has to stop the madness, either by reducing the degree of reprisal, or ending the relationship entirely. As Mr. Gandhi says, "An eye for an eye only ends up making the whole world blind."

Consistency

Trust is closely aligned with consistency. If a person's actions match their words and they are predictable, then, therefore, they are consistent. Generally, you can trust such people to be who they say they are. People who are inconsistent can't be trusted because you don't know what they're going to do next. Sometimes their feelings and actions are real, and other times they're not. Now sometimes the opposite is true: people stay with liars because they know that trait to be consistent, and they've decided to live with it. But inconsistency, and the instability accompanying it, will drive you insane. They cause stress and distress. You will never know that person, and if you don't know them, you can't be connected to them. You can recognize consistency because of your knowledge of people. We're back to knowledge.

I have known people who seemed incapable of telling the truth; they would lie even when the truth would have served them better. They seemed to be afraid of the possibility of anyone getting to know them. But a major part of connecting and loving is knowing; you can't have one without the other.

———•◆•———

34
CHAPTER

Compromise

You may have been told that compromise makes relationships work: social, business, and love. We like to urge our co-workers, our political leaders, and our children to compromise. But what does that word mean?

For example, how do we decide what to eat for dinner? If I want Chinese food and you want Italian, how do we resolve this seeming impasse? Some would say compromise. But how would that work? We could eat Italian today and then keep track of our choice, so I get my desire next time. But, seriously, will we even keep track of it? Or will we have this conversation all over again next time, maybe even disagreeing about whose turn it really is? So maybe our "compromise" ends up being a third choice which neither of us really has a taste for. Do we flip a coin and let chance decide? Do we buy both, fix two dinners or get take out, so each of us gets what he wants? People spend much too much time and energy thinking about, debating, or attempting to change those things they actually have no control over. This is a waste of time and effort. At the same time, this arguing robs you of the time and energy you could be putting into activities or ideas you do have control over, efforts you can change.

Apply "compromise" to your values and it becomes a more profound but no less vexing question. Should you change your views concerning how to save the environment due to the views of your partner? Should you alter your belief in the goodness of people because your partner thinks everyone is evil and greedy? Can you live with yourself if you change your views about where the couch should sit in the living room? How important is the issue? There is a useful current saying: "First, don't sweat the small stuff; second, it's mostly small stuff."

Would you, should you, compromise in the area of abuse, perhaps accepting some amount, either in intensity or frequency?

Compromise or Collaborate?

The concept of compromising one's self is detrimental to the individual and, therefore, to the relationship. The act of compromising is a lose-lose situation because both sides feel they are giving into the demands of the other party. Over time, this continued compromise sets the stage of always giving in, feelings of being taken advantage of, which may lead to the feeling of, or actually being taken for, granted. This compromise rarely, if ever, achieves harmony. We simply both end up feeling cheated. Collaboration, on the other hand, is the act of working together. It is mindful, a proverbial win-win. As compromise is the evil twin, collaboration is the good twin.

Clearly, some ideas are not open to compromise such as your physical and mental well-being, your ideals, or the foundation of who you are. But whether you should eat Chinese or Italian is not a foundational aspect of who you are. Compromise is possible. However, try thinking about compromise from a different perspective. The problem with the act of compromise is it causes the person who thinks he's compromising to feel frustrated and perhaps think he's being taken advantage of. Ideally, both people should be compromising; however, since we don't know to what extent the other person is compromising, or if they are at all, there is always the possibility we are being taken advantage of. Actually, though, the person who feels she is compromising the most—losing the most by being gracious or responsible—simply assigns a greater importance to the issue. If the idea on the table isn't important to you, then you're not actually compromising. It simply doesn't matter that much. If the issue isn't important, it doesn't even make sense to label the process of exchange as compromise.

Coach Stephanie McKenzie points out, "There's a difference between having a challenge and forcing the relationship to work. Someone I know hates his wife. He's into the marriage and two kids later. There's a difference between 'we have a few things to make work' and 'we're oil and water.' If you're oil and water, then accept it and move on. If you're mayonnaise and all mixed together, it works. Sometimes you have challenges; that is how relationships grow and become stronger."

Compromise or Settle?

Let me clarify the words "compromise" and "settle." When we say compromise, we think the negotiation is positive, when we say settle we think it negative. But one aspect of compromise is "not getting what you want," and one aspect of settling is "not getting what you want," so there is no difference between the two.

Situations can be set up in three ways: "win-win," "win-lose," and "lose-lose." But only "win-win" or "lose-lose" are acceptable outcomes for a team, a relationship. "Win-lose" benefits only one person and, therefore, is not a reasonable outcome.

What is the definition of a win? Is it getting everything you want? Does it have no negative aspects? Or is it simply getting something you want and accepting any negatives that come along? Is a win a positive or simply the lack of a negative? Is it a win to come in first or not to come in last? Do those labels even matter if your own goal was simply to finish?

We say we want to "win," that is our most beneficial outcome. However, if both parties cannot win, then one party's win is an insult to the other party. In the case in which both parties cannot win, then it is better for both parties to lose, that is, compromise or sacrifice equally.

In one study, the premise is you are given $1 million, but you must share your winnings with a stranger. You get to decide how much to give, but the stranger can reject the offer. If he/she rejects, you both get nothing. The logical thing to do would be to offer the stranger a small sum. If the stranger refuses, he/she gets nothing, so why wouldn't someone accept? But somewhere in your brain, you can predict the other person will allow emotions to take over. When this experiment is performed in a lab with real money, most offers less than twenty percent of the total are rejected. Give the problem to a computer and it will take anything above zero.

When we evolved, survival depended on relationships and status. The money offered to the other person is interpreted as your estimation of his status. If the other person accepts less than twenty percent, he feels inferior and disrespected. The person will lose status if he accepts, and you know this instinctively; that's why you offer more. The promise of revenge is one way human beings ensure fairness.

So, no, you shouldn't compromise, but you should remember this: "It's collaboration not competition."

———————

35

Relationship Reassessment

"Happily ever after" is what happens at the end of a fairy tale. Think about it: that phrase implies nothing else ever happens, and there are no challenges to overcome, which means you aren't growing, so things stay the same. That is a stagnant relationship. So as good as "happily ever after" may sound, it isn't realistic, reasonable, or even what you *really* want out of life. A real relationship, in real life, doesn't just end when you get the prize. Every day is a new day, so how can "happily ever after" apply? This sounds like a bit of fortune telling with a side of guarantee tossed in for good measure.

After saving the village, you want to look back at all of the dragons the two of you have slain and commiserate. You want to feel the bond of having come together when it was necessary, and you want to value the bond created. In other words, each hurdle the two of you overcome together strengthens your bond. Not having any hurdles makes for a stagnant, never changing, never growing situation. Just because you arrived at your destination doesn't mean the effort ends. In fact, isn't that when the real fun is supposed to begin? You didn't plan, pack, and travel to New York simply to sit in the hotel room.

You need to reassess your relationship on a regular basis. Remember that a relationship has an unwritten, unknown, unverified, contract. People don't always either say what they want or even know what they want. (I hope I can help you with that paradox.)

You started and continued dating, working for, or being friends with someone for some particular reason. Maybe you like who they are or what they stand for. This applies to the physical, emotional, intellectual, and ideals. But when you change or he/she changes, the implicit or explicit contract is broken.

We don't realize that we break contracts all the time, yet we expect the relationships not to change. This means you need to reevaluate, reassess, and possibly renegotiate, periodically. This assessment applies to all relationships: you should reevaluate what you want and what you are getting out of business as well as social relationships. For example, you renegotiate your salary from time to time as your duties or skills change. Just so, in the beginning of any relationship, you are learning about the relationship and the players; therefore, you should evaluate the relationship more often.

Reevaluation Schedule			
Years	Months	Weeks	Evaluate
	1	2	
	3		
	4	2	
	7	2	
1			
1	7	2	
2	7	2	Critical
4	3		
6	10	2	
11	1	2	
18			
20	1	2	

Usually, as time passes, and you are more comfortable with the relationship, you reassess less often. Certainly, should something catastrophic or at least significant occur prior to the next scheduled reassessment, then you should consider an interim evaluation.

As a part of the reassessment process, you consider both the positive as well as the negative. This time can be used to remember what is important to you and why you made the choice(s) you did. Why did you choose what and who you did?

The schedule of weeks, months, and years of reevaluation which I propose is on the previous page.

These are absolute values meaning they start at the beginning of the relationship. Notice you need to reevaluate the relationship before the three-year mark and then again just after the four year mark, since this is a critical time in relationships. This is not to say you should go back to the beginning of the relationship. You assess what you want at each point: both what you want out of and what you want to put into this relationship, right here, right now. If you're married with five children, don't judge your relationship from back when you were single. You need to live in the present, not the past because from here you must look to the future.

Of course, you must consider the other parties to the relationship and, remember, you don't know them as well as you think you do.

In reassessing, Coach Stephanie McKenzie recommends the SWOT analysis: stress, weakness, opportunities, and threats. "Any tool that keeps you objective I'm good with. Out of our weaknesses birth our opportunities and out of our stress births our threats. If you're looking at your weaknesses objectively you'll see the threats to your relationship. If you love only when you feel like it, only when it's easy, your relationships will all be short lived, and shallow, there will be no chance for growth. Promote yourself from janitor, cleaning up relationships, to hiring manager, building your relationships."

There are some general and obvious questions that you need to ask both yourself and the other person:

- Do I still want the same things I originally wanted from the relationship? If not, what has changed?
- Does the relationship still meet its original purpose? If not, what has changed? Think of the relationship purposes from the patterns. For example, if you need validation, are you getting it?
- Does the relationship provide for the growth of all of the members? If not, why not?

- Do the members of the relationship respect each other? If not, why not?
- If there are changes, or differences, to the relationship, do you want to or can you provide the effort necessary to correct the differences? Are the rewards worth the efforts?

So if you are satisfied, your satisfaction can:

- Improve
- Remain the same (unchanged)
- Diminish

By the same token, if you are unsatisfied, your satisfaction can likewise:

- Improve
- Remain the same (unchanged)
- Diminish

In all cases, you and your relationship partner must choose either to stay (continue) or leave (discontinue). This is best done by reevaluating the relationship on a regular basis, using a set list of criteria. Even good relationships need to be reevaluated and possibly reworked (tweaked) in order to maintain the overall health. And depending on the outcome of the evaluation, leaving or ending the relationship may be the best, healthiest option.

———————

36
CHAPTER

Myth — You Can Have Unconditional Love

The myth of unconditional love is prevalent in media, movies, and romance novels. People who want to be the recipients of unconditional love don't want to accept responsibility for their own actions. They don't want to have any boundaries placed on themselves. But everyone has conditions or what Coach Stephanie McKenzie calls "deal breakers."

As Shakespeare noted, "A rose by any other name would smell as sweet." Just because you don't call them conditions doesn't mean you don't have them. There is no such thing as "unconditional love." Conditions are preexisting criteria which demarcate that which is acceptable from that which is unacceptable.

Could you, would you, fall in love with a rock? What about falling in love with someone of a gender other than the gender you are attracted to? Despite your objections to the contrary, you have conditions: your primary or initial conditions are a living, breathing human being of a specific gender. Remember the section of this book dealing with your values? Those values, beliefs, ideals, limits, boundaries, morals, ethics, standards, rules are all conditions. Without them, you have no way of knowing whom to pursue and whom to leave behind. Conditions are those criteria by which you make decisions about your relationships.

For example, you shouldn't allow certain situations to occur in your relationships. Coach Stephanie McKenzie notes, "I was tweeting the other day and asked, 'What are your deal breakers?' Someone didn't know what that meant. [For example] as a society, we have set laws against physical abuse and it should be a condition that you set for yourself."

So we say to ourselves and to our loved ones, "I won't do this" (referring to an action, behavior, way of thinking). In other words, this is my own personal limit, and you can count on me not to do "this" to you or us: these are my morals, my ethics, my values, my conditions. Conditions are necessary so I am held to some standard. If I am not held to any conditions, then I am capable of doing anything, including hurting you.

In addition, if you do not hold me to any standards or conditions, then how can I be sure you actually care for or about me? The more I do to get a reaction, attention, affection, out of you, and the more you let me get away with—that is, hold me to no conditions—the less I'll believe you are interested in me. In fact, this abusive view point, taking advantage of the other person, is nothing more than a spoiled child wanting to get his or her own way, regardless of others. This is merely acting the exploitative or martyred victim.

For example, on two separate occasions, two different women cheated on me. When I confronted them with their unfaithfulness, each asked me, "Don't you love me unconditionally?" My response to each was, "What about your love for me?" I had to assert some conditions for maintaining or quitting the relationships. Their love for me had not been bound by morals, ethics or values which were contiguous to mine and, therefore, their conditions for loving me were not the same as my conditions for loving each of them. They wanted to receive unconditional love, yet neither was willing to give it. It was entirely one-sided.

The book *Science of Influence of Persuasion* reveals that people have to demonstrate a certain amount of commitment, have certain standards, in order to be accepted. For example, when you join a club, you have to meet certain conditions in order to be admitted. Please don't confuse having standards, both for yourself and for others, with having to "prove" one's self to someone. Remember the section on Romantic Love's beginnings? If someone was aloof, the lover had to prove his love to her, the beloved must stay aloof to be worthy of the love, and so on. These are bizarre, unrealistic expectations. Being forced to prove yourself is a control mechanism, a manipulation technique. It is self-aggrandizing arrogance. Having standards—we might call them "conditions"—for yourself and for others represents a respect for your beliefs and values.

Too Many Conditions

Of course, one can set too many conditions which the other person cannot possibly meet or they pay attention to the insignificant conditions. Coach Stephanie McKenzie notes, "That's the problem that I start to see; that people set too many conditions. He didn't do this or that. People will accept the physical and emotional abuses, but won't accept things like you want Chinese and I want Italian and that's a deal breaker. They flip the important conditions for the unimportant conditions. People reverse the importance. Make little things big things to sabotage. I watched this person at fifty-one years old be with her baby daddy [for] twenty years, and I watched them have a knockdown fight over the level of gas she left in car. But she's still upset that he won't marry her. If you're going to fight, be fighting over important things. You don't fight for the things that matter because you don't know how to fight for the conditions."

People who want to be the contributor of unconditional love don't hold the other person responsible for their own actions. They don't want to place any boundaries on the other person. They are not only willing, but desirous of being misused, abused, and degraded. They feel themselves unworthy or undeserving of affection or attention. This represents low self-esteem.

The Importance of Conditions

Since conditions are limits, boundaries, and standards we hold others to, we need to be clear about the importance of having them and the necessity of following them. If a person is not held to any conditions, then he or she is capable of doing anything, including hurting others. In this way, allowing others to take advantage of you—by not holding them to standards—is a self-abusive stance. In terms of "actors," as discussed earlier, this person is an enabler, giving others whatever they want, regardless of whether it is good for the individual or not.

There are serious ramifications when one allows himself to think he's practicing unconditional love. A kind, loving woman told her story to me: she had one child with another on the way. One day, the police showed up at her door looking for her husband. They were about to arrest him for inappropriate acts with a minor. He admitted to these crimes and went to jail. She wanted to leave him but was undecided. Friends, many religious, made her feel guilty for questioning his commitment and being uncertain about her own actions. They claimed they could get past his problems. They said she should love him regardless of what he had done, that is, unconditionally. But she felt uneasy about this line of action. She thought he ought not to have committed these crimes and should have been taking care of her and their family. She finally got the help she needed from a Christian psychologist, who set her mind at ease, took her feelings into account, and explained that a relationship takes effort on the parts of all those in it, not just one or the other.

The Paradox of Unconditional Love

If you love me unconditionally, you'll let me get away with anything. But when will I be satisfied that the unconditional love has been proven? If you even so much as question anything I do, then is that a loss of unconditional love? Does the unconditional love have to be constantly tested? Will you need more and more bizarre, outrageous antics in order to be assured the love is truly unconditional?

The demand for unconditional love is a way in which we sabotage our relationships. When it's not perfect, the demander of unconditional love says, "You don't love me." The underlying modus operandi is "I'm going to keep testing you until you step away and then bemoan that you don't love me unconditionally." If you test someone who doesn't know he's being tested, he's doomed to fail.

Anything given too easily is of little value; in fact the value, other than monetary, is a combination of the supply, rarity, and demand, in other words what we need to do to earn or deserve a thing. So the conditions we place on both getting and giving of love are exactly what gives love its value.

"Unconditional love" and "neglect" masquerade as the same thing. "How is that possible?" you may ask. From the outside, unconditional love appears as approval or sanction of one's actions. But neglect also has no sanctions; that is, no one actively disapproves. The two non-actions can actually appear the same.

However, I know if you care for me, you'll hold me to some standard or condition, that is, love me conditionally. Coach Stephanie McKenzie says: "Especially with women, older women, they've come up with lovely traps because they've made all these lovely promises. 'I'm never going to do this again.' When it doesn't work out, they say no one can love them. They need MacGyver to navigate the way to love them. They want to be loved with no responsibility of their own. [It] shouldn't be assumptive. [It is] not okay for you to do something even if they might forgive you.

Maintain Boundaries

If you claim to set boundaries, and then you don't abide by them, that is, hold to them, then you've set yourself and your loved one up for failure. You may lament that you can't keep your boundaries or conditions because you think you should love or be loved unconditionally. But if someone sets bizarre conditions, like desiring perfection, a savior, I want you to fix me, or mind-reading, that's setting up for failure as well.

Whereas unconditional love would require no forgiveness, conditional love requires forgiveness. However, forgiveness is a process. (See chapter titled "Forgiveness," later.) You can't forgive someone who hasn't asked you for forgiveness. The first step is the acceptance of responsibility for the situation or the effect of the situation on the other person. A person who doesn't feel as if they have done anything wrong won't ask for or even want forgiveness because he or she has no remorse. The next step is to make amends in some way: this may be a material replacement or emotional sympathy. Lastly, the individual must make an honest, earnest, effort not to repeat the same circumstances.

If forgiveness is given too freely, too easily, and without any retribution, it won't be of any value. What is the motivation to change our behavior, as there is no cost? Why shouldn't we just keep doing what we are doing again and again? The false, easy, forgiveness rhetoric comes from the offenders themselves, those who want to be free to continue their transgressions.

Forgiveness and apology are directly related because they refer to the person who has been offended.

Don't be "Sorry." Apologize.

Sorrow is the feeling of only one person, not both. As such, sorrow doesn't accept responsibility, it doesn't make amends, and it makes no attempt to be restrained. "I'm sorry" is an expression of how you feel; it is all about you. It is not an expression of empathy which takes the other person's feelings into account. Grammatically, we cannot say, "I'm sorry to you." However, we can say, "I apologize to you." An apology is a process having multiple steps which have to be carried out before forgiveness can be received or given.

The truth is there is no such thing as unconditional love. NO such thing. Unconditional is theoretical, not practical. Therefore, people want, by either giving or receiving, something actually unattainable, even damaging. That is dysfunctional thinking.

Unconditional love is mainly associated with intimate relationships. However, it can just as easily be applied to friendships, family relationships—parents often speak about loving their children unconditionally—and business relations. How is unconditional love related to business? Some employers—and employees—believe people should be eternally grateful for their jobs and paychecks. They believe employees should do whatever is asked of them without question. This amounts to an unconditional adherence or loyalty. But it often backfires.

We need limits and boundaries to protect and preserve all people and all relationships.

37
CHAPTER

Myth — Relationships are Hard Work

Don't let anyone tell you relationships are "hard work." This is another myth of the advice-giving industry. If relationships were a job, you'd find another job. If you felt that love and friendship were constantly and overly difficult, you'd find other friends or other relationships. You'd be better off finding a job you enjoy which is rewarding, rather than expending huge amounts of effort for non-reciprocating, inconsistent or unequal, rewards.

In fact, relationships are supposed to be things you want to be involved in, not things that you have to be involved with. Jogging takes effort, shoe shopping takes effort, but if you enjoy something, it doesn't feel like "hard work"—effort, yes—"hard work," not at all. Even as far as effort is concerned, you hardly notice it.

I'm not saying relationships don't require effort, but it is just reasonable effort; even fun requires effort. The impression that fun happens spontaneously and without any effort is false. However, neither relationships nor fun should be "hard work." They both have to be rewarding, worth the effort.

If you think of your relationship as "hard work," you begin with a defeatist attitude, from the position of "Can I even do this?" Most people don't want to "work hard," they want to put in a reasonable effort and receive a reasonable reward, whether that is a relationship or fun.

One clue you can depend on: if you dread waking up in the morning to go to work, find another job. If you dread spending time with a person, find another relationship.

The Problem with Traditional Marriage Vows

The oldest traditional wedding vows can be traced back to the manuals of the medieval church. In England, there were manuals of the dioceses of Salisbury (Sarum) and York. The compilers of the first Book of Common Prayer, published in 1549, based the marriage service mainly on the Sarum manual. They are religious in nature, yet they are not biblical. They were created by men, hundreds of years after the Bible. Again this shows that the modern view of romance and love which we take for granted, as in the wedding vows, are only about 560 years old.

Are traditional marriage vows sabotaging your relationship?

The wording of the vows is vague and extremist. They aren't practical, meaningful or measurable, allowing for no exceptions. The type of attitude expressed in the vows seems to be in direct conflict with Scriptures, as extremes are considered to be sinful: wrath, greed, sloth, pride, lust, envy, and gluttony.

First let us focus on "for better, for richer, and in heath:" who in their right mind would end a positive relationship? All of these items are "a no brain-er." If you can't deal with the good times, then what kind of a relationship are you looking for? These items are so blatantly obvious as not to need mentioning.

At the other extreme is "for worse, for poorer, and in sickness:" these items set false, unrealistic, and unreasonable expectations. For example when "or worse" becomes physical or mental abuse, things have gone too far. How bad is "bad enough"?

The same extreme is evident in "for poorer." When poverty is self-imposed due to behaviors such as gambling, taking drugs, over shopping, excessive materialism, and so on, that is gluttony. Similarly the lack of motivation, under-earning, living well below one's potential, is sloth. How poor is "poor enough"?

When "sickness" is self-imposed, or the refusal of care, it's beyond the other person's duty or obligation. You can't force another person to seek or accept help. How sick is "sick enough"?

For example, I dated a woman who, unbeknownst to me, had a problem with alcohol. When we met, I had no reason to think of the way she drank as an issue. After dating for five or six weeks, I had noticed and assembled enough of the clues to realize she was an alcoholic. She had done a good job of hiding, excusing, apologizing, and denying the sickness. However, neither was she ready to make a change nor was I ready to deal with the long recovery process. Simply put, we did not have a long-term investment in the relationship which could justify such a commitment.

There have to be limits, boundaries, deal breakers. If not, you're asking for unconditional love, which is at best detrimental and at worst dangerous. Would you sign a contract that had no limits, or which was so extreme and vague that you couldn't possibility live up to the agreement?

The marriage vows are not a substitute for an investment in a relationship; they do not take the place of, or reduce, the learning process.

The wedding is neither the "beginning" nor the "end." The beginning of the relationship is when you met; the end is when you are no longer together. The wedding is simply one milestone in between.

———◆———

SECTION III

Detours Along the Route

39
CHAPTER

Love — What Is It, Really?

My definition or description of love is general. Just as we can generally describe a car, which allows you to spot many cars, a description doesn't need to be specific enough to single out your own car. The word love itself is often overused or misused. We love everything from cars, to food, to clothes, to shoes.

The way I see it, we can approach the concept of love from two ways or levels. Love for humanity, love for your fellow man, is a distant love, a broad, societal definition. But love of family and friends is a close love, a narrow, specific, individual definition. With every degree or variation between those two extremes is a potential defining point. Often, people don't differentiate between these levels, or degrees, of love, which creates confusion and leads to misunderstandings. Occasionally, a person "confuses" the two in order to manipulate someone. For example, someone says, "I love you," knowing full well that what he or she means is a love for humanity, but anticipating that you will interpret it as personal.

The Elements of Love — Knowing, Sharing, Caring

The first element of love is knowledge. We love that which we know—or what we think we know, or imagine, or want to believe. People often say, "To know them is to love them." However, varying degrees of knowledge exist, from a broad to a narrow knowledge.

Broad, general knowledge is a shallow, generic way of knowing. For example, we know and can relate to the fact that people have basic needs and feelings, both physical and emotional. We see the similarities of the group rather than the differences of the individual. You might think of this as public knowledge, things anyone might know.

Narrow, specific knowledge pertains to a deep and exclusive way of knowing. The more personal and private information someone divulges, including secrets, the more special we must be to be entrusted with it. This is private knowledge, things not just anyone knows.

With each new piece of information you discover, you must make a decision: accept it, reject it, or ignore it—feel indifferent or ambivalent. However, accepting does not imply agreeing with the action or feeling. We may accept a person who eats vanilla ice cream or thinks Twinkies are nutritional—after all, we all have some differences— without actually agreeing with the individual. Knowledge reigns supreme because the more we know about each other, the better we are able to define our connection. If an item is important to you, and you accept it, you will get closer and you'll like or love each other more. Twinkies go on the grocery list! The item becomes additive, beneficial, leading to a stronger bond. But if an item is not significant to you, or it's redundant to what you already know, then it neither benefits nor damages the bond. You may like strawberry ice cream, but it's not important that your beloved loves vanilla. Such a situation represents the majority of items between people.

However, if something is important to you, and you reject the other person's like/dislike, you will move apart and you'll like or love each other less. In such a case, the item becomes detrimental, leading to a weaker bond.

Occasions occur when knowledge can put an end to love. Should you find out the person you are in love with has either been deceitful or he or she has acted in a way you find repulsive—you discover your beloved is a thief, a murderer, a pedophile—your loving feelings will be severely affected.

The second element of love is sharing. Just as with knowledge, varying degrees of sharing exist, from the protected through the unprotected. In fact, sharing relates closely to knowledge because you cannot know that which isn't shared.

Protected sharing refers to a restricted, carefully controlled sharing. When people guard themselves and the items they share, they can manipulate others' view of them. Sometimes protected sharing has more to do with the person's personality. He or she may be wary of sharing for various reasons.

Unprotected sharing is open, unrestricted and trusting. Often, sharing of this kind concerns those things or feelings others either don't know or aren't interested in knowing.

Sharing shouldn't be confined to the grand things in life, such as raises and promotions, which we share with almost anyone; but it also shouldn't be limited to our deep dark secrets or our embarrassments. Sharing the mundane, seemingly insignificant day to day occurrences greatly influences love.

The third element or level of love is caring, which depends on both knowledge and sharing. You can't care about the things you don't know about and haven't shared. Like knowledge and sharing, varying degrees of caring exist, from the superficial through the invested. The less we know, the less we can empathize, and the less we empathize, the less we are willing to do. The more we know, the more we are able to empathize; the more we empathize, the more we are willing to do.

Superficial caring involves a limited investment of time or effort. You care, but not quite enough to do very much or go very far out of your own way; you do what you can or want to without putting yourself out.

Invested caring means unrestricted, requiring time, effort and sacrifices. You are not only willing but enthusiastic about the prospect of caring. As you will see, caring can be measured in quantity and quality of time spent, effort exerted, and sacrifices made.

For example, I had been dating a woman for a long time. One day I noticed her car headlight was out, so that weekend I went to the auto parts store to buy a replacement light. I went to her house to install it. She wasn't grateful; instead she told me repeatedly that I shouldn't have bothered. I was surprised and taken aback by her reaction. I didn't realize then she was rejecting my caring. I found out later around that very time she was either already involved with someone else or contemplating it.

<table>
<tr><td>

Elements of Love

Knowledge — amount
Sharing — degree
Caring — quality
Bonding — intensity

</td></tr>
</table>

Knowledge, caring, and sharing combine to create connections and bonds. The extent of the connections varies in intensity based on the amount of knowledge, the degree of sharing, and the quality of caring.

Testing the Definition of Love

How does the definition relate to these common statements: "I love you, but I'm not in love with you" or "I love you like a brother/sister"? This is love in a general, generic way. It's like saying, "I know some things about you that I like, and some things I don't;" or "I know some things about you I accept, and some things I don't;" or "I know some things about you which I flatly reject." In these cases, we don't have enough in common; we don't share the same values or goals. The individual feels he has shared as much as he is willing to or as much as he feels comfortable sharing. The caring cannot go any further because the individual doesn't care enough to invest of his or her self, to give you the time, effort or sacrifices, which you either expect or which this type of relationship requires. The person feels some kind of connection or bond; however, it isn't as strong as this relationship requires or it isn't the right type of connection for this relationship. The individual doesn't feel connected, passionate, desirous about you or about the two of you.

Does this definition apply to "love at first sight"? When someone says he's fallen in love "at first sight," he's saying something like the following: "I very much like what I know about you already, even though it isn't very much;" "I'd like to share things about myself with you, and I'd like you to share things about yourself with me;" "I am willing to give you some of my time and energy and make certain sacrifices for you, which is to say I care about you;" "I feel a connection or bond with you. I'm drawn to you, like a moth to a flame."

At this point, we're imagining what the other person is like, or what we want him or her to be like. We think we know. This instant attraction or connection can occur in any type of relationship, such as between new friends or even new business associates. You just click or hit it off. It is immediate and intense. You identify with, relate to, and have an appreciation for the other person. Any, or all, of these things can either build or diminish over time.

Love at first sight isn't an assurance of a lasting love. When love at first sight doesn't last, we revise our history. We say things like "It wasn't actually love at first sight," or "It was only lust," or "If this feeling had been love at first sight, the relationship would have lasted." That last comment is a reversal of cause and effect. Don't be fooled into thinking that "Love at First Sight" is somehow stronger, more special, or a more "real" love. We cultivate or grow love.

So what does it really mean when we say "I love you"? If you love your shoes, and you use the same phrase to describe your feelings for me, what am I to think? Just as shoes can be bought and owned, can I be "owned"? Just as shoes are worn only when you feel like it and left in the dark the rest of the time, can I be taken out and used whenever you feel like it? Just as shoes get worn out and are discarded to be replaced with a newer, better pair, can I be so easily replaced?

You can see it is actually insulting to use the same word to describe what could be a deep, meaningful human relationship and just about everything else in your life. If a word is used to describe everything, then it doesn't describe anything. This misuse of the word "love" may contribute to people not knowing what love is or why they can't recognize it when they see it or why they can't express it when they feel it.

Love is a transaction. It takes two. For example, if I offer you twenty dollars, and you don't accept it, then I haven't given it to you. I've made an offer of my love, but it hasn't been accepted. If the receiver accepts or allows himself to be loved for the wrong reasons or under false pretenses such as self-interest, then it is fraudulent, deceitful, dishonest, and possibly even abusive. This cannot be considered real or true love.

I used to believe refusal or rejection of caring should be simply attributed to coy demeanor, shyness, modesty, reservation, a sense of manners. However, I have found when people either refuse or are uncomfortable accepting caring gestures, it is often because they don't want to give it back. They feel they are accepting gifts under false pretense, without the desire of reciprocating.

By the same token, love accepted for the right reasons is love likely to be returned in kind, favored. We feel compelled to reciprocate when we willingly, honestly, receive caring and kindness. This kind of love, which is returned, should be accepted for the correct reasons as well.

As the definition suggests, love is knowing, sharing, caring, and bonding. Therefore, if someone knows, shares, cares, and bonds with you, and you accept it, and you know, share, care, and bond with them, and they accept it, then you have created a cycle, a completed transaction, of love.

It is Easier to Give than to Receive

The Four Phases in the Cycle of Love

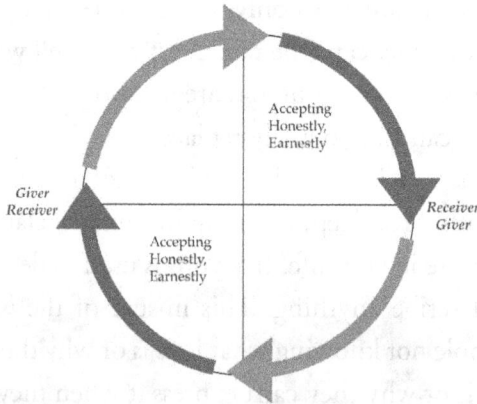

One-sided feelings are infatuation, not love.

We cannot force our love onto someone, we cannot force them to accept our love, we cannot force them to return our love, and they cannot force us to accept their love.

This is where people have the most problem. Love is circular, like a wedding band, and as such there is no clear beginning and no clear end. In that way it is not truly clear where love starts, who is the giver and who is the receiver. This version also shows why love cannot be between, or does not include, inanimate objects, unable to either accept, or return love.

When reassessing your relationship, a good exercise is to write down all of the ways you both give and receive your love. Then exchange your notes with the other person in the relationship. You may be very surprised to find that what you are giving as well as what you are getting, and what they are accepting and what you are accepting, aren't the same. In other words, you may find that what you are giving, as a sign of you caring, is not being seen or accepted, in the way you intended and vice versa. You may care more or less about each other than either of you actually realizes.

Misused Words Destroy Love

A word which is of importance to love but which is often misused and misunderstood is "want." What does it mean to want? We use the word "want" repeatedly during our day. Our parents were quick to point out the difference between wants and needs when we were children; however, they didn't fully explain the two different uses, or meanings, of "want."

When we say we want to do something, or go somewhere, what do we typically really mean? This use of "want" generally implies we are curious or intrigued. When we tell our manager we want a raise, the manager understands that means an investment of time, energy, and sacrifice. Therein lies the confusion: when we tell a person we "want" something, he or she typically believes it to be the latter, an investment of time, energy, and sacrifice, when in truth it is nothing more than curiosity.

We have no intention of taking the time, expending the effort or making the sacrifices necessary to actually do what we say. When we say, "I want to be with you," "I want the relationship to work," or even, "I want a relationship," if we are not willing to invest the time, expend the effort, or make the required sacrifices, then we aren't being honest. We may be intrigued, curious, or simply wishful; however, we aren't motivated and actively pursuing the steps necessary to achieve these goals. Typically, we are saying there is something we don't want—such as solitude—but we aren't willing to do anything about it other than make statements to the opposite effect.

Adding to our definition of love, we have a combination of wants or desires: that is, time, efforts, and sacrifice, coupled with the investment of fame, fortune, and favors. Fame represents not general celebrity but rather local individual admiration. Both fortune and favors are relative to one's own socioeconomic situation. Fortune and favors are some of the physical, more obvious measures of time, effort and sacrifice.

There has to be a "give and take." In business, the employer provides the fortune (the pay), and the employee provides the favors, the work or services. In friendships, in certain circles, one person may be the "popular one," having a kind of local fame, whereas others may be more of the "doers," the ones who make most, if not all, of the outing plans and arrangements; they are the facilitators, the favors. In all relationships, we each have our strengths and our weaknesses; we contribute our strengths and rely on the strengths of others, collaboration.

Love must be built incrementally. Just as a literal investment, it would be unwise to give too much too soon without some collateral. Yet that is exactly what we do, at least that is what I have done in the past. We accept an "I.O.U." or promissory note, and we make bad investments. We give more than we get, with the hopes of hitting it big and recouping all of our losses. We don't all have the same amounts of time, effort, sacrifice, fame, fortune, or favors; therefore, we must balance what we give with what we are getting in return. If I have an abundance of time to give, you may need to reciprocate with your excess fame, the stature you have in our community, our circle.

The Four Phases of the Cycle of Love

The Four Phases in the Cycle of Love

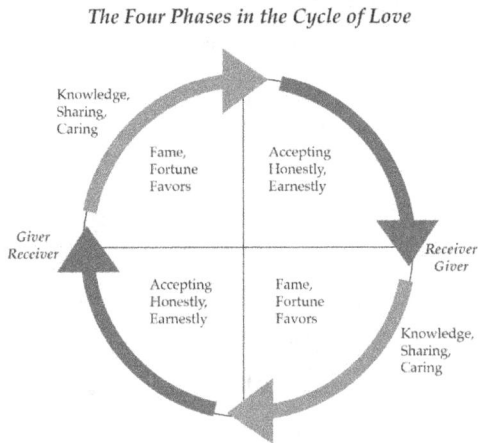

How are love and happiness related? What is happiness? Can we define it?

There are three tenants of happiness:

- A place to be, (home, work, charity, somewhere).
- Someone who wants you there, even if it is only yourself.
- Something of meaning, something that makes a difference, something valuable, worthwhile, to do while you are there. In other words, consistency (stability), appreciation (relationship), and a feeling of self-worth.

Many self-report studies point to various causes for the end of a relationship, among them finances, physical intimacy, and so on. These are nothing but the symptoms of a relationship that was already in distress.

I'll say it again: by far the greatest impediment to any relationship is lack of knowledge. Not knowing what you yourself want, not knowing what the other person wants, not knowing the purpose of the relationship all lead to the dissolution of the relationship. In the same way, thinking you know what you want when those wants are contradictory or mutually exclusive creates an unattainable, unachievable, scenario, a relationship that cannot, and does not, exist.

For example, you may want to be with someone who is physically appealing, yet you don't consider the time, effort, and sacrifices the person makes in order to achieve and maintain that appearance. You may want to be with a highly motivated, successful individual, yet you want that person to spend all of his or her time with you, not pursuing passions outside of the relationship. You may want to be lavished with gifts, attention and affection, yet you want your own time apart. You may want excitement, yet you are afraid of trying anything new.

The so called "Golden Rule"—give unto others as you would have given unto you—is, in fact, inadvisable and won't help love along.

For example, I heard about a long-married couple who struggled for months in their relationship and finally went to a marriage counselor for advice. After listening to the couple's complaints, the counselor suggested each person select a night on which he/she would treat and pamper the partner in the manner they wanted the partner to treat them. The wife treated her husband first. On a Tuesday, the husband arrived home to a quiet house to find fresh rose petals spread across the floor, creating a path leading to the bedroom. On the bed lay a soft velour robe and a hand-written note which read, "Get comfortable, put this on, go in the bathroom, and enjoy!" In the bathroom, the husband found the jacuzzi tub filled with bubbles, ringed by scented candles. A large glass of wine and a thick romance novel sat on the edge of the tub. The following Thursday the husband took his turn. The wife arrived home with great anticipation to discover a six-pack of beer with a note. The note read, "Honey, the house is yours for the night. There is more beer in the fridge, hot wings are warming in the oven, and there is all the blue cheese and salsa you can eat. The big game is on tonight, and I ordered it for you on pay per view. The comfy chair, the big screen TV, and the remote control are all yours tonight! Don't worry about me and the kids; we will be watching the game at the sports bar down the street." How happy do you think each person was?

We know people have different needs, wants and desires. We also generally have the attitude people are individuals and unique; we are not all the same person. Therefore, this idea of "doing unto others as we want" is contradictory to what we actually know to be true. Moreover, it's a self-centered and selfish perspective, denying differing experiences, opinions and individuality. It views the world, and the people in it, strictly from the view point of "me and only me." It is disrespectful of the other person because it assumes they want what you want and feel the way you feel. Just because you might enjoy a warm bath has absolutely no bearing on what someone else may want or enjoy.

The true golden rule is to treat others as they themselves need and want to be treated; this requires time, effort, and sacrifice to understand what you can do for the other person. On your part, this amounts to caring and respect. "Do unto others as they need done, regardless of whether it is what you would need, or would want, done unto you." This isn't about people being from different planets. It is about people not knowing their partners: not taking the time to get to really know yourself or another, not sharing your wants or desires with each other, not caring enough to put in the effort required to support one another, and not making the sacrifices necessary to include others in your life.

Another misapprehension that destroys love is "It's the thought that counts." Not entirely.

It isn't just the few moments someone takes thinking about you which shows they care. It is the deep, specific, personal knowledge of you, your likes as well as your dislikes. It is the time one takes, both getting to know you in the first place, and the quantity and quality of that time spent, even though you are not together at that particular moment. It is the effort one expends on you, both while you are together and while you are apart. It is the sacrifices and choices you make that place you above something or someone else. "It is the time, effort, knowledge and significance that counts."

There are those who would joke you should never give a gift of function: "Never give a woman cooking utensils." But if the person in question is an aspiring chef, and the utensil is a set of professional knives, this gift shows a personal knowledge of that person.

If you don't know what gift to give someone, you demonstrate the lack of a personal, meaningful, connection with him or her. You haven't taken the time, invested the effort, or made a sacrifice to get to know your friend or lover. When a child crafts a gift by hand, that gift embodies the time spent on you, specifically, while apart, and the child's significant effort, the effort being measured from the child's point of view, the sacrifice of not playing, or doing other, more fun activities. Some adults tend to dismiss, and diminish, the caring by simplifying it to "Well, it's the thought that counts."

The phrase most often quoted gleefully by people is not even close to being accurate: "The best things in life are free." The best things in life cost more than any material accoutrements. Time is every person's most valuable "item." "Time is money," we hear, but you can't get a raise in your time, you can't get a second, or better, job to gain more time. Once spent, you will never get it back, no repayment, no interest. Therefore, it should be cherished, used wisely, and not wasted. Money can buy many good things; however, "Money can't buy love" or friendship or loyalty.

The best things in life, relationships, are those things you want; therefore, they cost time, effort and sacrifice. Oddly enough, our "significant" others are the people with whom we want to share the "seemingly" least significant things, which is exactly what makes these items significant. Of course, we can have more than one significant person in our life. The relationship we have with the person determines which "insignificant" items we share with them.

For example, my buddy Eric just recently started his own business. We talk regularly about business, both the good and the bad. Recently, Eric called, excited, to tell me some news. One of his clients had mentioned to him they were doing business with him particularly and not necessarily the company he was representing. He went on to say if Eric chose to change distribution, they would follow him because their relationship meant more to them than the product. Now this glowing compliment isn't something a person announces to the world. We don't shout it from the roof tops or put a banner on our web site. It isn't of public significance; it is of personal significance. Getting a new job, a raise or having a baby is announced to the world, but news of this kind is for sharing with a significant other.

This remark told Eric he had made the correct decision to launch his own business; his contribution was being valued. He was making a difference and other people noticed. This item is of business significance; therefore, Eric chose to share it with me. On the other hand, if you are made to feel that these items you are sharing are not being appreciated or meaningful to the other person, you'll stop sharing.

And when a person stops sharing, the existing bonds of the relationship begin to deteriorate, and new bonds are not made. It is simply a matter of time before the relationship ends in earnest. For example, I've been in relationships in which I shared some small, silly, part of myself, and I was made to feel foolish for expressing those thoughts or feelings. Had I known then what I know now, I would have understood this was a sure indication of a lack of interest in me and, therefore, the relationship. I think many parents, adults, and other authorities tend to do this to children, treat them as if their views are insignificant or irrelevant. Just because it doesn't mean the world to you, doesn't mean it isn't important to someone else.

It's important to note now you have an actual definition, even though high level, of what it means to create bonds, and now you can put measures to knowledge, sharing and caring, and the quality, quantity and depth of time, effort and sacrifice. Now you can begin to validate the extent of your relationships.

40
CHAPTER

Liars and Lying

When you lie, you steal the right and the ability to make a choice or decision from the person being deceived. It has been shown the liar uses more words on average than someone telling the truth, uses first person-singular ("I") less often, uses third-person pronouns more often ("he," "she," "it"), and has a slight but consistent elevation in negative terms and disparaging remarks. Will this help you catch a liar at work? Maybe. But the most important elements to understanding when someone is lying are knowledge and attention.

Who are you more likely to detect as lying, a stranger or someone you know? With the stranger, you are on guard: the stranger doesn't know you and, therefore, doesn't know what you might respond to, how to deceive you. But a person who knows you knows how to lie to you, and you are more accepting and comfortable, therefore, vulnerable, with that person. So, despite our best hopes, a person who knows you can more easily deceive you.

Nonetheless, liars are hard to spot. Research reveals surprisingly few valid cues of deception, and people with special training in security, like judges and police officers, often do no better than chance at spotting lies. Even polygraphs have been shown to be of no value in detecting liars, which is why they are not admissible in a court of law.

One of the ways to protect yourself from liars is to pay closer attention. People want what they want. For example, I wanted to be in a relationship, so I ignored some actions I should have questioned. Had I forged on, I likely would have either received an answer of "You don't trust me" or some sort of lie. In either case, I didn't want the confrontation. It's easy to lie to someone who "wants" to believe the lie; con artists rely on that.

Furthermore, people tend to judge others as they are themselves, so if you are honest, you expect honesty in return. You don't understand why a person would lie in any given situation.

But relationships require a certain degree of shared information; it isn't a relationship without it. Think of two strangers on the street. They don't have a relationship because they don't have knowledge of one another. Depending on the type and intensity of the relationship, there are different types and quantities of information that need to be shared.

Too many people take the attitude or accept the attitude of "This is none of your business because I'm entitled to my privacy." If you want to be "private" while in a relationship, then "go be private somewhere else." If you feel there is an issue of importance, then you have a right to ask. If your beloved has an issue with telling you what he or she is doing, then the two of you need to seriously reassess your relationship.

One time I was dating a woman, and from time to time I was uncomfortable with the relationship. I would want to be together and she would say, "I'm going out" or "I'm busy." I knew those were vague excuses. I realize now I should have assessed my involvement in the relationship; I should have been more awake and more aware. I didn't want to at the time, didn't want to ask questions and rock the boat. I wanted the relationship to continue no matter what because I didn't want to be alone, even though it wasn't good for me.

We can't prevent people from lying to us. All we can do is watch for the lies. Be willing to pay attention, ask questions, put in the required time, effort, make some sacrifices, and end the relationship if necessary.

————— ◆ —————

41
CHAPTER

Cheating

If you ask ten different people what it means to cheat, you will likely get ten different answers. Let's begin with a definition of cheating.

To cheat is to defraud or swindle; to deceive or influence by fraud; to violate rules or regulations. Cheating is intentional deception, both active, outright lying, and passive, acts of omission, in order to gain advantage, influence, or elude the accepted conventions or expectations, whether formal or informal, of a relationship. Cheating involves betrayal, the loss of trust. Cheating occurs in all realms of human life. If you believe cheating is strictly physical, sexual, then I never want to play cards with you.

You will discover when people get overly specific, or creative, when it comes to using the word "cheat" in regards to relationships, they are attempting to justify their own thoughts or desires. They themselves simply don't want to be judged as cheats. Because relationships involve not only the physical but the emotional and the intellectual as well, one can cheat without being physically involved. As I've noted before, don't believe the self-report surveys because people lie (cheat) even when reports are anonymous.

Let's use heterosexual relationships as the template. We have four categories to compare: married, single dating, single not dating, and those not interested in dating. By definition, every married male must be paired up with a female. Likewise, every dating couple is a pair of one male and one female.

We'll assume cheaters typically cheat with only one other person at a time. We are only interested in the total number of male versus female cheaters and not the number of their partners, so this is a reasonable assumption.

If a married male is cheating with either a married or a dating female, they are both cheating; therefore, as far as the number of cheaters is considered, they cancel each other out.

Additionally, if a dating male is cheating with either a married or dating female, they both are cheating; therefore, as far as the number of cheaters is considered, they cancel each other out.

Other males who are either married or dating are cheating with available (unattached) females. By the same token, the married, dating females are involved with married, dating or unattached males.

In order for there to be any significant difference in the number of men cheaters versus women cheaters, we would have to believe one of two possible scenarios: 1) many men are cheating with one, and only one, single woman or 2) there are enough single women (unattached) to accommodate all the cheating men. In addition, we'd have to completely ignore or disregard any single men who are with married or dating women (the women in this case are the cheaters, not the men).

None of these scenarios is realistic: there isn't a single wanton woman, and there aren't enough single women (remember, not all cheaters are cheating with singles, and single men most certainly do have relations with married or dating women). Furthermore, by answering the question "Who do people cheat with?" we can easily see the relationship status of the affair partner doesn't have anything to do with the fact of entering into the relationship, thereby making that a non-issue as a criteria for cheating.

Who Do Men Cheat With?

Men cheat with married, dating, or attached females for some obvious reasons. There is less of a chance of attachment; therefore, there is less of a commitment. There is the mutual risk, which means less of a chance of being caught and exposed. There is the accessibility or opportunity: if you travel in the same circles, it is easier to meet and justify spending time together. Because you are already friends, you already have some things in common. Also, your guard may be down since one or both of you are already in a relationship, so your friendship presents a less threatening atmosphere, allowing for a greater level of comfort and familiarity.

Of course, all of these conditions are the same for females, so there is no gender-based difference for this group. In other words, the question "Who do women cheat with?" is answered in the same way.

People already in a relationship are more likely to know how to attract other relationships because, after all, they already know how to navigate the nuances of their primary relationships. People who already have a job are more likely to be hired by an employer than those who are unemployed.

The Other Side of Cheating

Several surveys show a far greater number of men cheat than women. So why don't the numbers add up? This is, in fact, another arena in which men and women aren't different from one another.

One factor in the skewed numbers is that self-report surveys and studies are much less reliable than previously thought. People are not truthful either intentionally or unintentionally. Several studies indicate this phenomenon.

Another factor is what I'll call the sympathy vote: the person who has been cheated on rarely gets the empathy he or she deserves as a victim of the crime of cheating. I'll call into the record my own experiences. When I spoke to people about my having been the victim of a cheating lover, the first thing I heard from both men and women was, "What did you do?" A close second was, "What didn't you do?" In other words, it was my fault that I was cheated on. This is no different from blaming any victim of a crime: it was your fault you got, robbed, raped, beaten, and so on. It was in your control not to let that action happen to you and you did.

Another thing I heard from both men and women was, "You must not have satisfied her," implicitly or explicitly suggesting I was insufficient as a sexual partner. This attempt to emasculate me certainly worsened my feelings of distress. And lastly I heard from women, "Well I was cheated on by a man, so it is just payback," as if the simple fact of my being a man meant I deserved such treatment. There was no sense I was an individual who had personal feelings.

In all cases, I was met with contempt. I was looking for support and sympathy, only to find distance and anger.

I think it is for these reasons men don't admit to being cheated on, whereas some women speak more freely about it. In some cases, women know men are less likely to expose them, so they may feel empowered to get away with their indiscretions.

People are afraid of the topic of cheating because they, too, may be subject to it and its effects. We want to feel as if we have some semblance of control in our lives, especially when it comes to being cheated on. To accept that it wasn't my, the victim's, fault would be to suggest they, too, might fall victim to this crime.

"I'd Know if My Partner were Cheating on Me"

You'd know when? At the first glance, first kiss, first month? You can't know until "after" it has happened, so it is already too late. We all can find out at some point in time; however, the damage will already be done, and the pain will still be as great. What we do next, after we have found out, is equally as important as simply knowing. When we say we'd "know," we deceive ourselves in order to feel at ease.

People judge others as they are themselves. If you wouldn't cheat, you don't expect others to cheat on you, and vice versa.

Cheating with Strangers

Women who claim to want to connect with friends get more physically excited by strangers than friends. Strangers are more exciting than known men, according to Chivers' study. Is this really a surprise?

Should it be any different for men? The reasons are fairly obvious: we know our friends, know their faults or quirks, whereas strangers are whoever we ourselves make of them. We can imagine and fantasize anything and everything we want them to be, regardless of who they really are.

People often imagine what their partners can be in the beginning of any new relationship. We assume or wish what we want about the other person, regardless of what we actually know, or don't know, about them.

So Why Do People Cheat?

It is in our "nature" to cheat. For both genders, there are common reasons for cheating:

- Self-esteem, both low and high, and
- An inability to deal with the issues or conflicts of the current relationship.

Low self-esteem manifests itself in different ways. One way of boosting one's self-esteem, or measuring self-worth, is by being so desirable you are able to lure someone away from someone else. This action smacks of inadequacy or a sense of undeserving. The only way to prove to yourself, and others, you are worthy of a relationship is to take one from someone else. If I can take this away from you, I must be really good. My company must be better than theirs if I can lure their top performers away. Another way to show an increase in your own self-worth is by trading up, getting something better than what you have already.

One can cheat on a friendship or a business relationship by intentionally taking advantage of the situation through deception. How many of us have searched for and found another job while still working at our current position? It isn't uncommon. Your first job has trained and prepared you for the next, better job. Just so, your current relationship makes you feel you are better than you thought or, at least, good enough to do better. But in this situation, you have one foot in the door and one foot out of the door. You stay in one relationship while finding another relationship in order to supplement something you feel is missing, which you now think you deserve. At the same time, you avoid the risk of losing what you currently have. Sound familiar? Remember the possible Relationship Progressions?

Perhaps you are getting one thing from one relationship such as stability and or material benefits and something from the other relationship such as excitement or intimacy, affection, and attention.

High self-esteem indicates a sense of entitlement. Your needs, wants and desires are more important than those of others. This is a self-centered, self-important view. All that matters is getting what you want.

As you see, both a low self-esteem and a high self-esteem appear the same to the external observer.

The inability to deal with the issues or conflicts of the current relationship can be expressed in many ways.

First, if you think the current relationship or job is essentially over or unsurvivable, emotionally if not physically, then it appears to be in your own best interest to get as much as you can out of the situation before it finally comes to an end. You are trying for the best of both worlds. But this applies to you only and is, therefore, selfish. This is a hedging of bets, containing the least amount of risk. This situation has an element of low self-esteem because it indicates you are not confident you actually can find another relationship or job to take the place of this one. However, it may also be a case of the current relationship or job boosting your confidence to the level where you feel you can now do better.

Second, you may want companionship without the commitment. Why would you want companionship? After all you already have a companion. So this is a situation where you are avoiding the existing relationship and its issues. It is indicative of an inability to deal directly with conflict. You'd rather not spend time dealing with the tough issues at work; instead, you'd rather spend your time, effort, on the easy jobs, or maybe even non-work related projects.

Rather than either fixing or ending the relationship at hand, we find it easier to simply find a new relationship without the burdens. But it's a fantasy to think this new relationship will be effortless or stress free, the dream of perfection.

Of course, in some cases, looking for or getting another relationship may be a way to spur the end of the existing relationship. I firmly believe at least two of the times my girlfriends cheated on me, their sole purpose was to end our relationship rather than confront me or its issues. Combined with the "unconditional love" they insisted upon, they didn't have to take any responsibility for ending our relationship. I was the bad guy by ending the relationship, and it was me who didn't know how to love.

Third, you may be envious of the other person's existing relationship. This feeling may come about because of low self-esteem, a lack of confidence in one's own decision-making process, a lack of individuality, or simply laziness. We have a tendency to believe if the other person accepts you, then you must be good enough for me; you are, essentially, pre-screened. If that company employs you, then I want to employ you, too.

By the way, the easiest way to judge how a person will act in a relationship is to observe them *in* a relationship. People are who they are and will act certain ways regardless of the relationship. In other words, you don't need to see how someone is in a specific type of relationship. How do people interact in their everyday lives? How do they treat family, friends, and business relations? If a person steals from work, would you really be surprised to find they would steal from you, too?

I noticed one woman I was dating treated the wait staff poorly when we went out to eat. She was a waitress herself, so I didn't understand her condescension. She was self-centered with both family and friends. In the beginning of the relationship, I was on the inside of her circle; it was only a matter of time before I was an outsider, and she was treating me the same way. I overlooked the red flags and never thought her behavior to me would be the same. How many people want an attack dog and then are shocked when the animal bites them or someone they care about?

A fourth reason people look for other relationships while they're in one is vengeance or revenge either for having been cheated on, or for the perception of a slight so egregious that one desires to exact a significant, and deeply meaningful, retribution. If the company won't give me the raise I feel I deserve, I'll get something of value out of them another way. But this is passive-aggressive, inflicting harm indirectly, without taking ownership, responsibility, for your own actions.

Of course, many of these reasons for cheating may be combined and may be present, to different degrees, in relationships. As the reasons for cheating aren't gender based, there is no reason to believe one group is more likely to, or prone to, cheat. However, in general, people who are not happy in their current situation and choose to find a substitute or replacement elsewhere are lacking in communication skills. They can't articulate or clearly verbally express their needs and wants or, more likely, they themselves don't know. If they could, they would face their problems and either deal with them or, knowing they made a real and proper effort, end the relationship. They would simply move on and find someone or something new.

———◆———

42
CHAPTER

Trust Lost

It is true that trust is earned, which is to say consistent actions, coupled with matching words, over time, are the basis of trust. That said, what happens when trust is lost? What happens when the actions are inconsistent or when the words and the actions don't match? And more importantly, in the event that trust is lost, can it be re-earned? And if so, how?

If we begin from the position of trust and are faced with some deceit, what then?

- We need to discover the intent of the deceit: was it done with malice or simply born out of stupidity?
- We need to determine the extent of the deceit: was it a personal deceit, made against you specifically or was it more general, like an exaggeration?
- We need to define the occurrence of the deceit: was it the first, second, or third time? Once is a mistake; twice is a pattern.
- We need to decide the significance, importance, of the deceit, to us personally. All deceit needs to be taken seriously because it is only a matter of time before deceit of others becomes deceit to you and then deceit to self.

Deceit leads to the degradation of trust. Left unrectified, it festers and grows. The deceiver can either apologize, honestly and sincerely, or ignore the situation. The apology is an attempt at repairing the broken, lost, trust.

Should the deceiver apologize, you can choose to either forgive and move on, or not forgive. The forgiveness is an attempt at repairing the broken, lost, trust.

At each juncture, you and the other party have a choice to make: try to repair the trust or not.

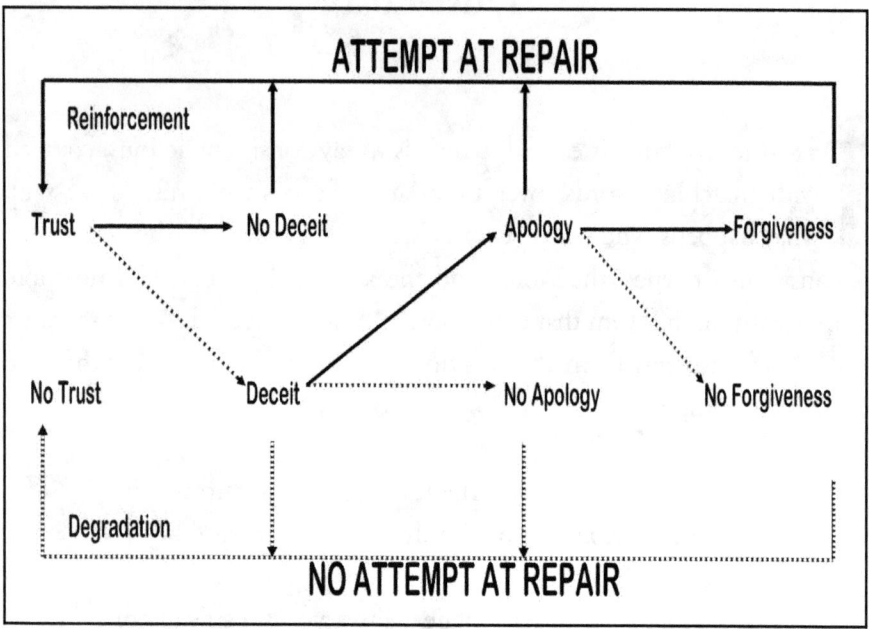

ATTEMPT AT REPAIR

Reinforcement

Trust → No Deceit   Apology → Forgiveness

No Trust   Deceit ⋯→ No Apology   No Forgiveness

Degradation

NO ATTEMPT AT REPAIR

43
CHAPTER

Forgiveness and Conflict Resolution

There are only four positions possible to resolve conflict.

1. **Work through it.** This is a transaction and, thus, requires two parties.
2. **Work around it.** This is a transaction and, thus, requires two parties.
3. **Move past it.** This is not a transaction; it requires only one party.
4. **Avoid it.** This is not a transaction; it requires only one party.

1. Work Through It

- Requires acknowledgment of the issue(s).
- Requires an apology, honest and earnest.
- The acceptance of responsibility for the situation.
- Restitution negotiation.
- An agreed upon restitution.

- At this point, and only at this point, may the apologist state whether the situation was unintentional, "I didn't mean to ... hurt you," "It wasn't my intention to ...," "I wasn't thinking when I ...," and so on.
- Too often this is where people start, so it becomes an excuse not an apology, as if to say, "Because I didn't intend to do it," it doesn't count or matter.
- Modification of behavior, attitude.

Working Through It, The Restitution Negotiation

- Begins with the apologist, offender, making an offer of restitution.
- This is necessary for buy in. I've had people come back after an apology and claim their apology wasn't real because they felt, forced, coerced, obligated, or guilty: "I only did this or that restitution, because you asked for it, not because I actually wanted to."
- The receiver of the apology must, and can, only direct the apologist as to whether the restitution is enough, or in kind; that is, whether he is headed in the correct direction, but you can't tell the other person what he is willing to give. What this means is that the receiver must know what he is willing to accept. This also allows the apologist to refuse if the receiver is being unreasonable or overly demanding.
- Therefore, they both must agree. Neither of them, the apologist nor the receiver can rightfully claim later that the other did not go far enough. There is no renegotiation after the fact.
- If one or the other does not agree with, or accept the

terms of the restitution, then there is no apology and no forgiveness.

Negotiation Tips

- It shouldn't be difficult to determine the restitution for a material object: replace it in kind, fix it, or pay the insurance deductible.
- Emotional offenses are more difficult to reimburse.
- First, the offender must hear out the emotions of the offended; that is not to say the offended gets to:
  - Be abusive, belligerent, obnoxious;
  - There is no yelling, screaming, or character assassination, no name calling.
- Instead the offended expresses her emotion by the use of "I" statements, as in,
- "I feel, hurt, deceived, disappointed, abused, used, embarrassed, offended. I didn't deserve to be treated this way," and so on.
- The offender should offer some sort of comfort, time, a handshake, eye contact, a hug, a shoulder to cry on, as appropriate as a show of solidarity with the offended. If the offender runs away, he isn't taking responsibility.
- The offender should avoid making, and the offended should not expect, unreasonable, absolute statements such as
  - I'll NEVER do that; that will NEVER happen again.
  - The offender sets herself up for failure, knowing that the promise is untrue, and possibly unreasonable; she can't live up to it, and so it becomes defeatist, "Since I can't be perfect, then what is the point?"

Although the apology may be negotiated and accepted, it is not fully satisfied until such time as the modification to the behavior, or attitude, has been satisfied. In other words, it will take time. Both parties need to realize and accept this, and have a reasonable time frame in mind as a part of the apology negotiation.

This conflict is a loss of trust, whether intentional or unintentional, although it may be less so if unintentional. The trust will have to be rebuilt, re-earned, which will take time, patience, and continued adherence to the negotiated resolution. Any future, similar violation of the resolution must be viewed not as a new, singular event but from the point of a repeated pattern. This is why it is not forgotten: we learn from our past, both positive and negative, thus to forget means not to learn.

At some point, the conflict must be placed in the past, the apology and forgiveness complete. Although not forgotten, you both have to decide to move past it, get over it, move on with your lives, because that is what you both agreed to do.

2. Work Around It

- Requires acknowledgment of the issue(s).
- Requires a partial apology, honest and earnest.
- A partial acceptance of responsibility for the situation.
- Restitution negotiation.
- An agreed upon, partial, restitution.
  - At this point, and only at this point and not sooner, may the apologist state if the situation was unintentional, "I didn't mean to ... hurt you," "It wasn't my intention to ...," "I wasn't thinking when I ...," and so on.
  - Too often this is where people start, it becomes an excuse not an apology. As if to say, "Because I didn't intend to do it," it doesn't count or matter.
- Partial modification of behavior, attitude.

Working Around it, The Restitution Negotiation

Is the same for Working Through It, with the addition, or understanding that:

- A complete resolution cannot be reached or agreed to; however, the restitution should be adequate.
- Both parties agree to accept the partial agreement, accepting that neither of them is getting entirely what they would have liked.
- The relationship continues, but it is altered; things will not, cannot, remain the same between the two of you.

Again, although the apology may be negotiated and accepted, it is not fully satisfied until such time as the modification to the behavior, and or the attitude, has been satisfied. In other words, it will take time. Both parties need to realize and accept this, and have a reasonable time frame in mind as a part of the apology negotiation.

This conflict is a loss of trust, whether it is intentional or unintentional, although it may be less so if unintentional. The trust will have to be, at least partially, rebuilt, re-earned, which will take time, patience, and continued adherence to the negotiated resolution. Any, future, similar violation of the resolution must be viewed not as a new, singular event but from the point of a repeated pattern. This is why it is not forgotten; we learn from our past, both positive and negative, to forget means not to learn.

At some point the conflict must be placed in the past, the partial apology and partial forgiveness complete. Although not forgotten, you both have to decide to move past it, get over it, move on with your lives, because that is what you both agreed to do.

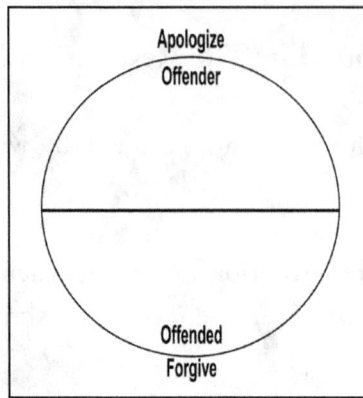

3. Move Past It

- One party feels there are issues while the other does not.
- There is no apology, and, therefore, there can be no forgiveness.
- We need to face this fact, as it happens often.
- In this situation what we must do is
  - Acknowledge the other person will not take responsibility. We cannot force another person to accept responsibility for his or her actions;
  - Acknowledge our own feelings and emotions;
  - Voice your "I" statements, aloud, to yourself, possibly in a mirror;
  - Accept this is the end of the relationship, either entirely or, at the very least, partially. The other person is not who you imagined, hoped, she was.

This conflict is a loss of trust, whether it is intentional or unintentional, although it may be less so if unintentional. The trust cannot be rebuilt. The relationship is ended, or altered significantly. At least we have learned something of the other person, as well as of ourselves.

At some point, the conflict must be placed in the past although it will not be forgotten. You have to decide to move past it, get over it, move on with your life, without the other person's involvement. You are not a bad person. You just need to get on with your life. Anything less allows the other person to infect and degrade your personal happiness.

Forgiveness is not the means by which a person moves on from a conflict. The opposite of Love is Hate, both of which require effort; therefore, they are both a part of caring. The opposite of caring is indifference. You don't need to love or hate another person. The true measure of moving on from a conflict is by not harboring any ill will, or negative feelings for, or towards, the other person. In this case we must practice indifference: "I don't allow you to influence my actions, occupy my thoughts, interfere with my emotions, or use any of my resources, as they are mine, and mine alone."

That is not to say "Forget;" it is to say, "Remember without caring." This position retrieves any hold, or power, the other person may have had over you.

Most people misuse forgiveness, due to the blame game. This is a part of the Dichotomy Model of opposites, "right versus wrong," "true versus false," "good versus evil," "Madonna versus Whore." It assumes when someone is wronged, hurt, or offended, the other person is to blame, and therefore that person needs to apologize and ask for forgiveness and be forgiven.

There are situations where one or both people are, or feel, wronged, hurt, or offended, and it isn't a case of blame, or placing fault, in which case there is no need for either apology or forgiveness.

If your relationship partner decides to end the relationship without anger or malice, you and they may have feelings of sorrow, yet there is no fault, no blame. It may be the right decision, and so there is no apology, no forgiveness. The two of you must simply "move on."

You can't give that which wasn't requested or accepted. You cannot forgive a person who has not asked for forgiveness. You may offer forgiveness; however, if it isn't accepted, then you haven't actually given anything. Indeed, some people may be offended by your forgiveness because forgiveness implies an offense has been committed.

If I go into your purse and remove twenty dollars, you may be tempted to forgive me. I, on the other hand, may only be taking back what is rightfully mine: I loaned you that twenty dollars six months ago, and month after month, you have nothing but excuses as to why you won't pay me back. I don't want your forgiveness. As a matter of fact, I am offended you fault my actions because you are trying to make yourself appear righteous and pious when you are far from it. I am not asking for, nor do I want, your forgiveness.

I have had more than one woman tell me that she would forgive me for getting upset with her for cheating on me if I would forgive her the cheating. No. I am well within my rights to be upset, and I have done no wrong.

4. Avoid It

- This decision requires nothing.
- Sadly, it is the most common position for conflict, and yet it is the one position that should never be utilized.
- We avoid apologizing, taking responsibility, or seeking an apology, which is holding the other person accountable for his actions.
- Since there is no apology, no forgiveness, and no challenge, there is no resolution.
- In some, maybe even many, cases one party never even knows there is a conflict. Therefore, they can't take responsibility, make restitution, or modify their behavior, attitude.
- The conflict is allowed to fester, grow, and poison the relationship.
- This leads to the cycle of greater conflict and possible explosions, instead of resolutions, which leads to more avoidance.
- In time, the relationship sours and ends, either, figuratively or literally.

———•—•———

44
CHAPTER

The Road Map

So where do we go from here? Any subject affecting virtually every aspect of a person's life and extending from birth to death is significant and vast. It isn't possible to capture such a large and important subject in a single book or movie.

This book is just the tip of the iceberg. I assure you I have a great deal more information and other topics to discuss, so please visit my website regularly.

www.GoodTogether.com
www.JerryBrook.com

———— •◦•◦• ————

SECTION IV

Appendix

References

As I pointed out in the beginning, it has been a number of years, a number of varied topics and a number of books and articles that have led me to these conclusions. I have found insight, some good some bad, in almost everything I have read. Therefore, it would be of no benefit to list every book and article or reference each individual page. However, following are some references that stood out and might be helpful to you.

Amen, Daniel G. M.D. *The Brain in Love: 12 Lessons to Enhance Your Love Life* July 14, 2009

Bergner, Daniel. *What Do Women Want?: Adventures in the Science of Female Desire.*

Berne, Eric. *Games People Play: The Basic Handbook of Transactional Analysis.*

Carnegie, Dale. *The 5 Essential People Skills: How to Assert Yourself, Listen to Others, and Resolve Conflicts* (Dale Carnegie Training)

Cialdini, Robert B. *Influence: Science and Practice* (5th Edition)

Dixit, Avinash K. and Barry J. Nalebuff. *Thinking Strategically: The Competitive Edge in Business, Politics, and Everyday Life.*

Edwards, Dilwyn. *Guide to Mathematical Modelling.*

Freedman, David H. *Wrong: Why experts* keep failing us—and how to know when not to trust them *Scientists, finance wizards, doctors...* (June 10, 2010)

Hancock, Jeffrey T., Lauren E. Curry, Saurabh Goorha, and Michael Woodworth.

"On Lying and Being Lied To: A Linguistic Analysis of Deception in Computer-Mediated Communication." Discourse Processes. Pdf source

Harris, Judith Rich. *The Nurture Assumption: Why Children Turn Out the Way They Do.* New York. Free Press. 1998

Hockenbury, Don H. and Sandra E. Hockenbury. *Discovering Psychology.* 5th edition.

Hogan, Robert, John Johnson and Stephen Briggs (eds). *Handbook of Personality Psychology.*

Hunt, Morton. *The Natural History of Love.*

Kirschner, Rick. *How to Click with People: The Secret to Better Relationships in Business and in Life.*

Levitt, Steven D. and Stephen J. Dubner. *Freakonomics: A Rogue Economist Explores the Hidden Side of Everything.*

Lilienfeld, Scott. O., Steven Jay Lynn, and John Ruscio. *50 Great Myths of Popular Psychology: Shattering Widespread Misconceptions about Human Behavior.*

Lynch, Carmen M.F.C.C. & Victor Daniels. *Relationship Gestalt: What Movie Are We in?*

McRaney, David. *You Are Not So Smart: Why You Have Too Many Friends on Facebook, Why Your Memory Is Mostly Fiction, and 46 Other Ways You're Deluding Yourself.*

Neuwirth, Erich and Deane Arganbright. *The Active Modeler: Mathematical Modeling with Microsoft Excel.*

Rosenthal, Edward C., Ph.D. *The Complete Idiot's Guide to Game Theory.*

Saaty, Thomas L. *Fundamentals of Decision Making and Priority Theory with the Analytic Hierarchy Process.* (Analytic Hierarchy Process Series, Vol. 6)

Taylor, Kathleen. *Brainwashing: The Science of Thought Control.*

Weintraub, Walter. *Verbal Behavior in Everyday Life.*

Wilson, Glenn D. and Chris McLaughlin. *The Science of Love*

———————